YOUR recipe could appear in our next cookbook!

Share your tried & true family favorites with us instantly at

www.gooseberrypatch.com

If you'd rather jot 'em down by hand, just mail this form to...

Gooseberry Patch • Cookbooks – Call for Recipes
PO Box 812 • Columbus, OH 43216-0812

If your recipe is selected for a book, you'll receive a FREE copy!

Please share only your original recipes or those that you have made your own over the years.

Recipe Name:

Number of Servings:

Any fond memories about this recipe? Special touches you like to add
or handy shortcuts?

Ingredients (include specific measurements):

Instructions (continue on back if needed):

D0912165

Special Code: **cookbookspage**

Over ➤

Extra space for recipe if needed:

Tell us about yourself...

Your complete contact information is needed so that we can send you your FREE cookbook, if your recipe is published. Phone numbers and email addresses are kept private and will only be used if we have questions about your recipe.

Name:

Address:

City: State: Zip:

Email:

Daytime Phone:

Thank you! Vickie & Jo Ann

Gooseberry Patch

An imprint of Globe Pequot
246 Goose Lane
Guilford, CT 06437

www.gooseberrypatch.com

1•800•854•6673

Copyright 2021, Gooseberry Patch 978-1-62093-451-7

Photo Edition is a major revision of *Mom's Favorite Recipes*.

Do you have a tried & true recipe...

tip, craft or memory that you'd like to see featured in a **Gooseberry Patch** cookbook? Visit our website at **www.gooseberrypatch.com** and follow the easy steps to submit your favorite family recipe.
Or send them to us at:

Gooseberry Patch
PO Box 812
Columbus, OH 43216-0812

Don't forget to include the number of servings your recipe makes, plus your name, address, phone number and email address. If we select your recipe, your name will appear right along with it...and you'll receive a **FREE** copy of the book!

Table of Contents

butter

brown sugar   1 t. cinnamon

Gently toss apples   9" pie crust

cinnamon

pie crust

sugar and

on the

topping

apples

kitchen of

Grandma

spiced cake Mix

cooking oats, uncooked

OPTION:
1 c. chopped n

packed

Recipe Cake Mix Brownies

½ c. margerine

50 caramels

5 oz. can evap. milk

9¾ oz. pkg. German

9¾ oz. pkg. German Cake Mix

Dedication

Dedicated to moms
everywhere...the best cooks we know!

Appreciation

Our heartfelt thanks for sharing
your best family recipes!

Egg Casserole

1 lb. Sausage, cooked
4 eggs, beaten
6 slices white bread, cub
½ c.
2 c. ched
ated

Recipe for: Perfect Pie
From: Lynn Stew
3 C. Flour   1 tsp. salt
1 Tbls. sugar
1 C. plus 2 Tbls. Butter
½ C. cold water
        white vinegar   3 crust

Outta bed, Sleepyhead!

in' Almond Coffee Cake. Serves 12
n the kitchen of— Jean Smart

_____s, beaten
butter
c. sugar

itermilk P___
milk
1 t.
½ t.
1 T. s
lender; blen___
skillet; hea___
t until gol___
Serves 2 - 3

Sharon Murray

Pecan Sticky Buns

½ c. milk
½ c. sugar
1½ t. salt
¼ c. margarine

½ c. warm water
2 eggs
2 pkgs. yeast
4½ c. flour,
divided

Scald milk in saucepan; remove
heat. Stir in sugar, salt
_____ide to cool.

Buttermilk-Cornmeal Waffles

Arlene Smulski
Lyons, IL

*Spoon some orange marmalade or strawberry preserves
between two waffles for a delicious filling!*

3/4 c. all-purpose flour
1/4 c. cornmeal
1 t. baking soda
1/2 t. salt

1 c. buttermilk
1 T. oil
2 egg whites

Combine the first 4 ingredients in a large mixing bowl; set aside. Stir buttermilk and oil together; set aside. Blend egg whites in a dry mixing bowl until stiff peaks form; set aside. Mix buttermilk mixture into flour mixture; blend until smooth. Gradually fold in egg whites; pour by cupfuls onto a hot, greased waffle iron. Heat according to waffle iron manufacturer's instructions. Makes 4 servings.

Passing along a thimbleful of flower seeds to a friend makes a cheery gift. Place them inside plain envelopes, and then bundle several envelopes together with vintage ribbon. You may even get a return envelope of seeds as a "thank you!"

Outta bed, Sleepyhead!

Strawberry Bread

Terry Kokko
Parris Island, SC

Since this recipe uses frozen strawberries, it's easy to enjoy any time of year!

3 c. all-purpose flour
2 c. sugar
1 t. baking soda
1 t. salt
1 t. cinnamon

4 eggs, beaten
1-1/4 c. oil
2 10-oz. pkgs. frozen
    strawberries, thawed and
    chopped

Combine the first 5 ingredients; make a well in the center. Set aside. Mix remining ingredients together; pour into flour well. Stir until combined; divide batter and spread into 2 greased and floured 9"x5" loaf pans. Bake at 350 degrees for one hour; cool in pans for 10 minutes. Remove loaves from pans and place on wire racks to cool. Makes 16 servings.

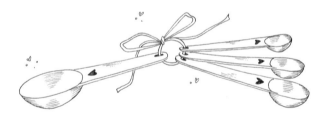

Sunshine in a Glass

Julie Shaw
Clovis, NM

A real pick-me-up in the morning!

1 c. frozen orange juice
    concentrate, partially thawed
1/2 c. milk

10 to 12 ice cubes
1 t. vanilla extract

Place ingredients in a blender; blend until smooth. Makes 2 servings.

Cheesy Potato Bake

Holly Corey
Burien, WA

I love serving this for brunch...a hit with family & friends!

32-oz. pkg. frozen diced
    potatoes, thawed
1 c. shredded Colby Jack cheese
10-3/4 oz. can cream of
    mushroom soup
10-3/4 oz. can cream of potato
    soup

1/2 c. sour cream
1/2 c. mayonnaise
1-1/2 c. corn flake cereal
1/4 to 1/2 c. butter, melted
1/2 c. grated Parmesan cheese

Combine first 6 ingredients; spread in a buttered 13"x9" baking pan. Set aside. Toss remaining ingredients together; sprinkle over potato mixture. Bake at 350 degrees for 30 to 40 minutes. Serves 8.

While scavenging tag sales, look for a vinyl or leatherette handbag like Grandma used to carry. Using acrylic paints and acrylic sealer, it can get a spunky makeover in no time!

Outta bed, Sleepyhead!

Mushroom-Noodle Omelet

Jodie Hanks
Minot, ND

You can easily substitute buttered noodles if you have some left over from last night's dinner.

3 T. butter, divided
1/2 c. sliced mushrooms
8 eggs
1 t. salt
pepper to taste

1 T. fresh chives, minced
1 T. fresh parsley, minced
2 T. water
1-1/2 c. prepared fine egg
  noodles

Melt one tablespoon butter in a small skillet; sauté mushrooms until tender. Remove from heat; set aside. Whisk eggs, salt, pepper, chives, parsley and water together in a mixing bowl; stir in noodles. Melt remaining butter in a skillet or omelet pan; pour in egg mixture. Heat over medium heat until bottom begins to set; add mushrooms down the center of the omelet. Loosen sides of omelet; fold one side over the other, covering the mushrooms. Cover and heat until done, about 3 minutes. Slip onto a warmed serving plate; slice into quarters. Makes 4 servings.

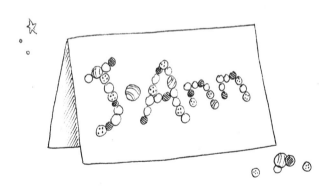

Vintage baubles and beads have so many uses... they add an extra-special touch to handmade cards, photo frames, placecards, pillows, memo boards or painted handbags.

Cranberry Scones

Cathy Light
Sedro Woolley, WA

I've had this recipe for so many years, it's a breakfast "must-have!"

2-1/2 c. all-purpose flour
2-1/2 t. baking powder
1/2 t. baking soda
3/4 c. butter, sliced

1 c. cranberries, chopped
2/3 c. sugar
3/4 c. buttermilk

Mix flour, baking powder and baking soda together in a large mixing bowl; cut in butter until mixture resembles coarse crumbs. Stir in cranberries and sugar; add buttermilk, mixing until just blended. Divide dough in half; roll each portion into an 8-inch circle, about 1/2-inch thick, on a lightly floured surface. Cut each portion into 8 wedges; arrange wedges on ungreased baking sheets. Bake at 400 degrees for 12 to 15 minutes; remove to a wire rack to cool. Drizzle glaze over the tops. Makes 16 servings.

Glaze:

2/3 c. powdered sugar
1 T. warm water

1/4 t. vanilla extract

Combine ingredients; mix well, adding additional warm water until desired spreading consistency is achieved.

Remember to tote a backpack on flea market adventures...it holds all the necessary goodies and keeps both hands free for shopping!

Outta bed, Sleepyhead!

Sweet Apple Butter Muffins
The Inn at Shadow Lawn
Middletown, RI

The center of each muffin is filled with a spoonful of apple butter...yummy.

1-3/4 c. all-purpose flour
1/3 c. plus 2 T. sugar, divided
2 t. baking powder
1/2 t. cinnamon
1/4 t. nutmeg
1/4 t. salt

1 egg, beaten
3/4 c. milk
1 t. vanilla extract
1/4 c. oil
1/3 c. apple butter
1/3 c. chopped pecans

Combine flour, 1/3 cup sugar, baking powder, cinnamon, nutmeg and salt in a large mixing bowl; set aside. Blend egg, milk, vanilla and oil together; mix into flour mixture. Spoon about one tablespoon batter into each paper-lined muffin cup; add one teaspoon apple butter. Fill muffin cups 2/3 full with remaining batter; set aside. Toss pecans with remaining sugar; sprinkle evenly on tops of muffins. Bake at 400 degrees until a toothpick inserted in the center removes clean, about 20 minutes. Makes one dozen.

Old-fashioned apothecary jars make the best vases. With their wide openings, they're just right for filling with an armful of just-picked blossoms!

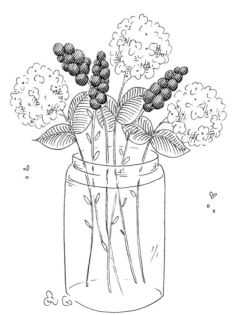

Golden Baked French Toast

RaNae Judd
Evanston, WY

A refreshing orange taste makes this anything but ordinary!

8 to 10 slices bread
1 c. milk
8-oz. pkg. cream cheese,
   softened
10 eggs

1 t. cinnamon
1 t. nutmeg
1 t. orange extract
1/4 c. brown sugar, packed
Garnish: warm maple syrup

Layer bread in the bottom of a greased 13"x9" baking pan; set aside.
Combine milk, cream cheese, eggs, cinnamon, nutmeg and orange
extract in a blender; blend well. Pour evenly over bread; cover
with aluminum foil and refrigerate overnight. Uncover and bake at
350 degrees until golden, about 35 minutes; sprinkle with brown
sugar. Drizzle with maple syrup before serving. Serves 8.

*Keep an eye open for clothespin bags...they're
usually in colorful vintage fabrics and are a handy
size for clever "in" and "out" mail totes.*

Outta bed, Sleepyhead!

Sausage & Red Pepper Strata

Lynette Mull
Newton, KS

A delicious layered casserole you make the night before.

6-oz. pkg. ground sausage
1/2 t. dried oregano
1/4 t. red pepper flakes
4 slices French bread, cubed
1/2 red pepper, chopped
1 t. dried parsley

4 eggs
1 c. evaporated milk
1 t. Dijon mustard
1/4 t. pepper
1/2 c. shredded sharp Cheddar
  cheese

Brown sausage with oregano and red pepper flakes in a skillet; drain and set aside. Line the bottom of a greased 8"x8" baking pan with bread; top with sausage mixture. red pepper and parsley. Set aside. Combine eggs, milk, mustard and pepper; whisk until well blended. Pour evenly over sausage mixture; cover tightly with aluminum foil and refrigerate overnight. Bake at 350 degrees for 55 minutes. Remove aluminum foil; sprinkle with cheese. Bake for an additional 5 minutes or until cheese is melted. Serves 4 to 6.

Its ideal shape and size make a woven berry basket terrific for filling with welcome bath treats and soaps for a guest room. If it's covered with a little flea market dust, just give it a quick rinse under cool water and let dry before filling.

Graham Cracker Breakfast Cakes

*The Governor's Inn
Ludlow, VT*

A favorite that warms us up on those chilly Fall soccer mornings.

3/4 c. all-purpose flour
3/4 c. graham cracker crumbs
1 T. baking powder
1/4 t. salt

1 c. milk
2 T. butter, melted
1 egg
1/2 c. chopped pecans

Combine first 4 ingredients; set aside. Whisk milk, butter and egg together; mix into flour mixture. Fold in pecans; pour by 1/4 cupfuls onto a hot, greased griddle or skillet. Heat until bubbles form along the edges; flip and heat until golden on both sides. Makes 8 to 10 servings.

Stitch a few whimsical charms, buttons or beads around the edges of a tea cozy...it will bring a smile every morning.

Outta bed, Sleepyhead!

Buttermilk Pancakes

Donna Behrens
Brookings, SD

I triple the recipe to feed my family of 6!

1 c. buttermilk
1 egg
1 T. sugar
1 c. all-purpose flour

1 t. baking soda
1/2 t. salt
1 T. shortening, melted

Combine ingredients in a blender; blend well. Pour by 1/4 cupfuls onto a hot, greased griddle or skillet; heat until bubbles form along the edges. Flip and heat until golden on both sides. Serves 2 to 3.

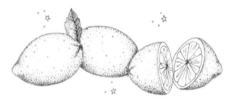

Apple-Lemon Pancakes

Donna Reid
Payson, AZ

*For a delicious crunch, sometimes I substitute 1/2 cup
chopped pecans for the lemon peel.*

2 c. all-purpose flour
2 T. sugar
2 t. baking powder
1/4 t. baking soda
1/8 t. salt
2 eggs, beaten

1-2/3 c. milk
2 T. plus 1 t. butter, melted
    and divided
1 apple, cored, peeled and
    shredded
1 T. lemon zest

Combine flour, sugar, baking powder, baking soda and salt; set aside. Mix eggs, milk and 2 tablespoons butter; add apple and lemon zest. Combine with flour mixture. Place remaining butter in a skillet; pour 1/3 cup batter into the hot skillet. Heat until bubbles form along the edges; flip and heat until golden on both sides. Repeat with remaining batter. Makes 12 to 16.

Come-on-Over Casserole

Cindi Rabon
Dalzell, SC

Just put this in the oven when friends drop by. What could be easier?

butter
12 slices bread, crusts trimmed
2 c. shredded Cheddar cheese
6 eggs, beaten

2 c. milk
1 lb. ground sausage, browned

Spread butter on both sides of bread slices; arrange slices in the bottom and up the sides of a greased 13"x9" baking pan. Sprinkle with Cheddar cheese; set aside. Whisk eggs and milk together; pour over bread. Crumble sausage on top; cover with aluminum foil and refrigerate overnight. Bake at 350 degrees for 45 minutes to one hour. Serves 6 to 8.

A day of "tag sale-ing" is much more fun with a group of friends. Check the local paper to see when the best sales are, call everyone up and make a date...you'll have a ball!

Outta bed, Sleepyhead!

Egg & Mushroom Bake

Debbie Foster
Eastover, SC

Topped with bacon and cheese, this will have 'em asking for more!

12 eggs, beaten and scrambled
8-oz. pkg. sliced mushrooms
10-3/4 oz. can cream of
   mushroom soup
2/3 c. milk
8-oz. jar bacon bits
1-1/2 c. shredded Cheddar
   cheese

Spread eggs in the bottom of a greased 1-1/2 quart casserole dish; top with mushrooms. Set aside. Combine soup and milk in a microwave-safe bowl; heat in a microwave oven on high for 3 minutes, stirring after each minute. Pour over mushrooms; sprinkle with bacon bits and Cheddar cheese. Bake at 350 degrees for 30 minutes. Serves 4.

Cheese & Chive Scrambled Eggs

Deborah Wells
Broken Arrow, OK

Served with bacon and biscuits, this is one dish we love so much I've even served it for dinner!

6 eggs, beaten
1/4 t. lemon pepper
1 T. dried chives
1/8 t. garlic salt
1 T. butter
1/3 c. shredded Colby Jack
   cheese
1/3 c. cream cheese, softened

Blend eggs, pepper, chives and salt together; set aside. Melt butter in a 10" skillet; add egg mixture. Stir to scramble, heating until set. Remove from heat; stir in cheeses until melted. Serves 3 to 4.

Almond Coffee Cake

Jean Smart
Coeur d'Alene, ID

During the holidays, add a cup of maraschino cherries for a cheery look and an extra sweet treat.

1/2 c. butter	12-oz. can almond pie filling
1-1/4 c. sugar	2 c. all-purpose flour
3 eggs, beaten	1 T. baking powder
1/2 t. vanilla extract	1/2 t. salt
1/2 t. almond extract	1/2 t. baking soda
1 c. sour cream	1/2 t. cinnamon

Cream butter and sugar; blend in eggs, one at a time. Add remaining ingredients; mix well. Pour into a lightly greased and floured Bundt® pan; bake at 350 degrees for 55 to 60 minutes or until cake springs back. Cool 30 minutes; remove from pan and cool completely. Serves 12 to 16.

Looking for a new message board? Hang an old-fashioned washboard for a whimsical way to keep notes organized! Just use magnets to keep messages and photos secure.

Outta bed, Sleepyhead!

Pecan Sticky Buns

Sharon Murray
Lexington Park, MD

Serve with a glass of icy cold milk for a winning combination!

1/2 c. milk
1/2 c. sugar
1-1/2 t. salt
1/4 c. margarine
2 pkgs. active dry yeast

1/2 c. warm water
2 eggs
4-1/2 c. all-purpose flour,
    divided

Scald milk in a saucepan; remove from heat. Stir in sugar, salt and margarine; set aside to cool until lukewarm. Dissolve yeast in warm water in a large mixing bowl; add milk mixture, eggs and 2-1/4 cups flour. Blend until smooth; knead in remaining flour on a lightly floured surface. Place in a greased mixing bowl; turn dough once to coat both sides. Cover and let rise until double in bulk, about one hour. Punch dough down; roll out on a lightly floured surface into a 1/4-inch thick rectangle. Sprinkle with filling. Roll up jelly-roll style; set aside. Spoon butter-nut mixture evenly into 12 greased muffin cups; set aside. Cut roll into 12 slices; arrange one slice in each muffin cup. Cover and let rise until double in bulk, about one hour. Bake at 350 degrees until golden, about 25 minutes. Invert onto a serving platter. Makes one dozen.

Filling:

1 c. brown sugar, packed

1/2 c. chopped pecans

Gently toss ingredients together.

Butter-Nut Mixture:

1 c. margarine, melted
1-1/2 c. brown sugar, packed

1 c. chopped pecans

Stir ingredients together.

Upside-Down French Toast

Victoria Hall
Bethesda, MD

Try using cinnamon-raisin bread for a new taste.

1/2 c. butter	8 to 9 eggs
1-1/2 c. brown sugar, packed	1-3/4 c. milk
1-1/2 t. cinnamon, divided	1/8 t. salt
8 to 12 slices bread	

Melt butter in a 13"x9" baking pan; stir in brown sugar and 1/2 teaspoon cinnamon, tilting to coat bottom of pan. Arrange bread slices on top; set aside. Blend remaining ingredients together; pour over bread. Cover with aluminum foil; refrigerate overnight. Bake at 350 degrees for 45 minutes; uncover and invert onto a serving platter. Makes 8 to 12 servings.

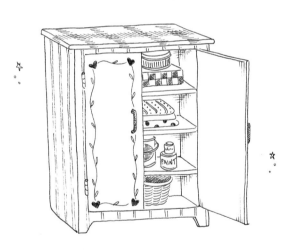

A secondhand utility cabinet is a good choice when looking for a craft cabinet. Invite friends to join in and help give it a facelift with acrylic paints. Everyone can swap stamps, stencils and painting tips while enjoying the time crafting together!

Outta bed, Sleepyhead!

Swirled Coffee Cake

Carol Doiron
North Berwick, ME

A boxed cake mix makes this a breeze to prepare!

18-1/4 oz. pkg. yellow cake mix
5-1/4 oz. pkg. instant pistachio
   pudding mix
4 eggs
1 t. vanilla extract

1 c. water
1/2 c. oil
1/2 c. sugar
2 t. cinnamon
1/2 c. chopped walnuts

Combine first 2 ingredients in a large mixing bowl; blend in eggs, vanilla, water and oil. Pour half the mixture into a greased Bundt® pan; set aside. Toss sugar, cinnamon and walnuts together in a small bowl; sprinkle half over the batter in the Bundt® pan. Swirl into mixture with a knife; add remaining cake batter. Swirl in remaining sugar mixture; bake at 350 degrees for 50 minutes. Cool and remove to a serving platter. Makes 12 to 15 servings.

A shadowbox is perfect for holding all those tiny trinkets collected over the years...charms, button cards, a school pin, souvenir matchboxes, pressed flowers or seashells. Each glance will bring back so many fond memories!

Chocolate Chip Waffles

Jo Ann

*No need for syrup, but top with a dollop of
whipped cream if you'd like.*

1-3/4 c. all-purpose flour
2 t. baking powder
1/2 t. salt
1-1/2 c. milk
1 T. butter, melted

1-1/2 t. vanilla extract
1 egg, separated
1 T. sugar
1/2 c. semi-sweet mini chocolate
    chips

Combine first 3 ingredients in a large mixing bowl; set aside. Whisk milk, butter, vanilla and egg yolk together until frothy; add to flour mixture, stirring well. Set aside. Blend egg white and sugar until stiff peaks form; fold into flour mixture. Gently stir in chocolate chips. Pour by 1/2 cupfuls onto a hot, greased waffle iron; heat according to manufacturer's instructions. Makes 6 servings.

Collect the colorful and vintage fabrics found at flea markets to use for a variety of craft projects... from a small stitched scissor keeper or pincushion to a larger friendship quilt.

Outta bed, Sleepyhead!

Double Chocolate Chip Muffins

Vickie

So rich and chocolatey!

18-1/4 oz. pkg. chocolate fudge
    cake mix
3.9-oz. pkg. instant chocolate
    pudding mix
3/4 c. water
4 eggs, beaten

1/2 c. oil
1/2 t. almond extract
6-oz. pkg. mini chocolate chips,
    frozen
Garnish: powdered sugar

Blend cake mix, pudding mix, water, eggs, oil and extract until smooth; fold in chocolate chips. Fill muffin cups 3/4 full; bake at 350 degrees for 25 to 35 minutes. Cool; sprinkle with powdered sugar before serving. Makes 2 dozen.

Color copy old textiles for one-of-a-kind photo or scrapbook album covers. Just copy the fabric, cut to fit the cover of a blank album and use spray adhesive to keep paper in place.

Sweet Mini Apple Dumplings

Karen Norman
Jacksonville, FL

Turn an all-time favorite into a bite-size breakfast treat!

2 8-oz. tubes refrigerated
    crescent rolls, separated
4 apples, cored, peeled and
    sliced into 8 wedges

1/2 c. butter
1 c. sugar
1 c. water
1/2 t. cinnamon

Cut each crescent roll in half, forming 2 triangles from each; roll up
one apple wedge in each triangle crescent-roll style. Arrange in a
13"x9" baking pan coated with non-stick vegetable spray; set aside.
Add butter, sugar and water to a small saucepan; bring to a boil.
Reduce heat; boil and stir until sugar dissolves. Pour over crescents;
bake at 350 degrees for 30 minutes. Sprinkle with cinnamon.
Makes 32.

The past is perpetual youth to the heart.
–L.E. Landon

Warm Apple Wraps

Sandy Rowe
Bellevue, OH

Try cherry pie filling too...yum!

21-oz. can apple pie filling
6 8-inch flour tortillas
1 t. cinnamon
1/3 c. butter

1/2 c. sugar
1/2 c. brown sugar, packed
1/2 c. water

Spoon pie filling evenly down the center of each tortilla; sprinkle with cinnamon. Roll up; place seam-side down in a lightly buttered 8"x8" baking pan. Set aside. Add remaining ingredients to a saucepan; bring to a boil. Reduce heat; simmer and stir for 3 minutes. Pour over tortillas; bake at 350 degrees for 20 minutes. Slice each in half and spoon juices on top before serving. Makes 12 servings.

Rummaging through a scrapbook or keepsake box
is sure to uncover an old snapshot that brings
a smile. Share the giggles...copy and send it off
to a friend in a greeting card!

Southwestern Egg Casserole

Michelle Witkowski
Shreveport, LA

If you want to make this the night before, just remove from the refrigerator and let stand 30 minutes before baking.

1/2 c. all-purpose flour
1 t. baking powder
1/8 t. salt
10 eggs, beaten
4 c. shredded Monterey Jack
    cheese

2 c. cottage cheese
1/2 c. butter, melted
2 4-oz. cans chopped green
    chiles, drained

Combine flour, baking powder and salt; stir into eggs, mixing well. Add cheese, butter and chiles; pour into a greased 13"x9" baking pan. Bake at 350 degrees until a knife inserted in the center removes clean, about 35 to 40 minutes; let stand 5 minutes before slicing. Serves 10 to 12.

The look and feel of secondhand linens is too irresistible to pass up! Stitch together 2 sides of a crochet-trimmed napkin for a perfect pocket to tuck jewelry in or use larger embroidered hand towels to hold treasured letters and cards.

Outta bed, Sleepyhead!

Zesty Brunch Quiche

Patty Schroyer
Baxter, IA

Try using peach or apricot salsa for a whole new taste.

9-inch frozen pie crust
1 c. shredded Cheddar cheese
4 slices bacon, crisply cooked
    and crumbled

2 green onions, thinly sliced
3 eggs, beaten
1/2 c. milk
1/2 c. salsa

Place pie crust in an ungreased 9" pie pan. Sprinkle cheese, bacon and onions into pie crust; set aside. Whisk eggs, milk and salsa together; pour into pie crust. Carefully place on a baking sheet; bake at 375 degrees for 35 minutes. Let stand 10 minutes before slicing. Serves 6.

Western-Style Quiche

Jennifer Upchurch
Junction City, IL

Serve with a side of hashbrowns for a stick-to-your-ribs dish!

12-oz. tube refrigerated
    buttermilk biscuits
8-oz. pkg. ground sausage
1/2 c. green pepper, chopped

1/2 c. onion, chopped
6 eggs, beaten
2 c. shredded Cheddar cheese
salt and pepper to taste

Arrange biscuits in an ungreased 13"x9" baking pan; set aside. Brown sausage with green pepper and onion in a skillet; drain and transfer to a large mixing bowl. Stir in eggs, cheese, salt and pepper; mix well. Pour over biscuits; bake at 350 degrees for 30 minutes. Serves 8.

Ham & Cheese Cups

Kathy Young
Beaufort, MO

Made in jumbo muffin cups, these make a hearty meal.

8-oz. tube refrigerated
   buttermilk biscuits
1 c. ham, diced
1/3 c. shredded Cheddar cheese

4 eggs
2 T. milk
1/2 t. pepper
1 t. dried parsley

Spray 5 cups of a Texas-size muffin tin with non-stick vegetable spray. Place 2 biscuits side-by-side, pressing dough up side of each cup to form a shell. Evenly sprinkle ham and cheese into each cup; set aside. Blend eggs, milk, pepper and parsley together; spoon evenly into each cup. Bake at 400 degrees for 10 to 15 minutes or until centers are firm; cool for 2 to 3 minutes. Makes 5.

Church Potluck tonight!

Jars of clothespins can be found for next to nothing at sales...glue them to memo boards to secure notes or photos.

Outta bed, Sleepyhead!

Early Morning Breakfast

Melissa Moser
Eureka, CA

This recipe needs to be chilled before baking...allowing time to look over the newspaper and make plans for the weekend tag sales, flea markets and auctions!

2 c. ham, diced
2 2-lb. pkgs. frozen shredded
   hashbrowns
1 T. green onion, chopped
1 c. shredded Cheddar cheese,
   divided

1 c. shredded Monterey Jack
   cheese, divided
3 c. milk
1 c. biscuit baking mix
4 eggs
salt and pepper to taste

Combine ham, hashbrowns, onion, 1/2 cup Cheddar cheese and 1/2 cup Monterey Jack cheese; spread in the bottom of a greased 13"x9" baking pan. Set aside. Combine milk, baking mix, eggs, salt and pepper; pour over hashbrown mixture. Top with remaining cheese. Cover; refrigerate for at least 4 hours. Uncover and bake at 375 degrees for 35 minutes; let stand 10 minutes before serving. Serves 8.

Use dots of craft glue to secure an old-fashioned button card to the front of a handmade card...so simple, but adds a lovely touch.

Cinnamon Biscuits

Deanna Brasch
Waterloo, IA

Dusted with cinnamon-sugar, perfect with a cup of tea.

2 c. all-purpose flour
1 T. baking powder
2 t. sugar, divided
1 t. salt
1/2 t. cinnamon, divided
1/4 c. butter
1 c. milk
butter, melted

Combine flour, baking powder, 1/2 teaspoon sugar, salt and
1/4 teaspoon cinnamon; cut in butter until crumbly. Stir in milk until
moistened. Drop by 1/4 cupfuls onto a greased baking sheet; brush
with melted butter. Set aside. Mix remaining cinnamon and sugar
together; sprinkle over biscuits. Bake at 450 degrees for 10 to
12 minutes or until golden. Makes about one dozen.

Scoop up holiday-themed postcards at tag sales;
they're so sweet and turn a plain jar candle into an
extra-special gift in minutes! Just color copy the
postcard, secure it to the front of a jar candle
using spray adhesive and it's done.

Outta bed, Sleepyhead!

French Market Doughnuts

Becki Quade
Paynesville, MN

Sometimes we frost and sprinkle with jimmies...excellent!

1 c. milk, scalded
1/4 c. sugar
3/4 t. salt
1/2 t. nutmeg
1 pkg. active dry yeast
2 T. warm water

2 T. oil
1 egg
3-1/2 c. all-purpose flour
oil for deep frying
powdered sugar

Combine milk, sugar, salt and nutmeg; set aside to cool to lukewarm. Dissolve yeast in warm water; add to milk mixture. Stir in oil and egg; blend well. Mix in flour; cover with wax paper. Let rise until double in bulk; turn onto a floured surface. Knead gently until smooth; roll out into an 18"x12" rectangle. Cut into thirty-six, 3"x2" rectangles; cover. Let rise for 30 minutes; place 3 to 4 at a time into hot oil. Remove with a slotted spoon when golden; drain on paper towels. Drop several at a time into a small brown paper bag; sprinkle with powdered sugar, shaking to lightly coat. Makes 3 dozen.

Keep a basket handy to fill with all those fabric snippets that are just too good to pass up. Before long there will be enough calicos to stitch into quilts or barkcloth to turn into curtains or pillows. The search is half the fun of flea marketing!

Simple Citrus Coffee Cake

Michelle Morole
Milford, DE

A hint of orange makes this extra special.

18-1/4 oz. pkg. white cake mix
1/2 c. warm water
1 pkg. active dry yeast
2 eggs
1/4 c. orange juice

1/2 c. all-purpose flour
1 c. brown sugar, packed
1 T. cinnamon
1/4 c. margarine, softened

Mix the first 5 ingredients together; pour half the batter into a greased and floured Bundt® pan. Set aside. Combine remaining ingredients; sprinkle over batter in pan. Top with remaining batter; bake at 350 degrees for 30 to 40 minutes. Invert onto a serving plate; drizzle glaze over warm cake. Serves 12 to 15.

Glaze:

1 c. powdered sugar
2 T. margarine, softened

2 T. orange juice

Gently mix ingredients together until smooth and creamy; add additional orange juice to reach desired consistency.

Use it up, wear it out.
Make it do or do without.

−New England Proverb

It's
Snacktime!

What's cookin'? Farmhouse Salsa
from: Debi Hansen

...ed tomatoes,
3 15 oz.
cho...
8 oz.
4 oz.
2 1/4 oz.
1 bun...
2 clo...
2 T.

Rec...
Stuffed Mush...
...ed spinach,
...d
1/4
1/4 w
1/2 t. d
1/2 t. dr

Recipe: Parmesan Tomatoes
From the kitchen of: Irene Robinson
5-6 tomatoes
1/2 cup sour cream
1/2 cup mayonaise
1/4 cup grated parmesan
1 t. garlic powder

Friendship Cheese Ball

Angela Nichols
Mt. Airy, NC

*I like to exchange recipes with friends and this one
has become a fast favorite.*

2 8-oz. pkgs. cream cheese,
   softened
5-oz. pkg. dried, chipped beef,
   chopped

1 T. mustard
1 T. mayonnaise
1/3 c. onion, chopped
1/2 to 1 c. chopped pecans

Combine first 5 ingredients together; shape into a ball. Roll in
nuts; wrap in plastic wrap. Refrigerate several hours before serving.
Serves 8 to 10.

*Turn a plain baby or toddler sweater into one that's
sweetly embellished...just add a vintage lace collar
around the neckline.*

It's Snacktime!

Golden Cheese Puffs

Robin Humberstad
Prosser, WA

Add a little more cayenne if you want an appetizer with a kick.

8-oz. pkg. cream cheese,
　softened
1/2 c. mayonnaise
2 T. onion, chopped

1/4 c. grated Parmesan cheese
1/8 t. cayenne pepper
1 loaf sliced party rye or wheat
　bread

Mix the first 5 ingredients together; spread on bread slices. Arrange on ungreased baking sheets; bake at 425 degrees until golden and bubbly, about 15 minutes. Serves 8 to 12.

Crunchy Bacon-Cheese Dip

Kelly Hall
Butler, MO

Just serve with bagel or pita crisps for a fast snack.

1 lb. bacon, crisply cooked and
　crumbled
4 c. shredded Cheddar cheese
1/2 c. chopped cashews

2 c. mayonnaise-type salad
　dressing
1 onion, chopped
Optional: chopped fresh chives

Mix all ingredients together; cover and refrigerate several hours before serving. Makes about 4-1/2 cups.

Farmhouse Salsa

Debi Hansen
Everett, WA

Stir in the chile pepper and jalapeño pepper juices
to really add some sizzle to this salsa.

3 15-1/2 oz. cans stewed
  tomatoes, chopped
8-oz. can tomato sauce
4-oz. can diced green chiles
2-1/4 oz. can black olives,
  chopped

1 bunch green onions, chopped
2 cloves garlic, chopped
2 T. rice wine vinegar
2 T. olive oil
4-oz. can jalapeño peppers,
  chopped

Combine all ingredients in a serving bowl; mix well. Cover with plastic wrap; refrigerate overnight. Serves 12 to 15.

Plain china or glass mugs are easy to find.
Create a one-of-a-kind set by adding polka dots,
stripes or names with acrylic permanent
paint...it's so easy and paintbrush clean up's a breeze
using just water.

It's Snacktime!

Hoboken Artichoke Dip

Lauren Bandman
Hoboken, NJ

So delicious! Serve with hearty slices of bread for dipping.

3 14-oz. cans artichoke hearts,
   drained
2 c. grated Parmesan cheese

1/2 t. cayenne pepper
3 cloves garlic, chopped
2 c. mayonnaise

Combine all ingredients; spread in an ungreased 13"x9" baking pan.
Bake at 350 degrees until golden and bubbly, about 30 minutes; serve
warm. Serves 12 to 15.

Slip a favorite photo in a pint-size charm photo
frame...so sweet on the front of a
family cookbook album or journal.

Sweet Onion Spread

Mary Beth Thiel
Doyline, LA

Top thick slices of sourdough or Italian bread with this
cheesy spread for a yummy and filling snack.

6 sweet onions, sliced
1/4 c. butter
1/2 c. prepared rice

2 c. shredded Swiss cheese
5-oz. can evaporated milk

Sauté onions in butter until tender; stir in rice. Add cheese; stir until melted. Spread into a greased 1-1/2 quart casserole dish; pour milk on top, mixing well. Bake at 350 degrees for 45 minutes. Serves 6.

Charms, hat pins, silver spoons or a locket are
all heartfelt treasures that belong together. Use
floral wire to gently secure them to a white-washed
grapevine wreath. A wonderful way
to spend the afternoon reminiscing.

Hot Pecan Dip

Jana Warnell
Kalispell, MT

Very simple yet elegant appetizer when served with baguette slices.

8-oz. pkg. cream cheese,
   softened
1 onion, grated
2 t. milk

3-oz. pkg. dried beef, chopped
1/4 c. green pepper, chopped
1/4 t. pepper
1/2 c. sour cream

Combine all ingredients together; mix well. Spread in a buttered 9" pie pan; sprinkle with toasted pecans. Bake at 350 degrees for 20 minutes. Serves 12.

Toasted Pecans:

1/2 c. chopped pecans
1/4 t. salt

2 t. butter

Toss ingredients together; spread on an ungreased baking sheet. Broil until golden; stir often.

Spend the day cutting and pasting! A vinyl overnight case from the thrift shop is easily transformed with acrylic paint and magazine cut-outs that have been decoupaged on. Protected with a coat of acrylic sealer, it's now a handy tote for Mom's makeup or teenage sleepovers!

Grape Jelly Meatballs

Karrie Earley
Martinsburg, WV

*Everyone should really try these...they're always a hit
with no leftovers.*

1 lb. ground beef
1/2 c. bread crumbs
1 egg
1 t. salt
1/2 t. pepper
1/2 t. seasoned salt
1/4 t. garlic powder

1/2 c. instant rice, uncooked
2 onions, minced and divided
2 T. brown sugar, packed
14-oz. bottle catsup
3/4 c. grape jelly
1/2 t. Worcestershire sauce

Combine first 8 ingredients; add half the onions. Mix well; form into
one-inch balls. Arrange in an ungreased shallow baking pan; set aside.
Heat remaining ingredients in a heavy saucepan until jelly melts,
stirring often; pour over meatballs. Bake at 325 degrees for
one hour. Serves 4 to 6.

*Old wool sweaters are easily turned into the softest
fabric. Just wash sweaters in hot water and then
place them in the dryer. Now they're ready to be
stitched into any variety of craft projects!*

It's Snacktime!

Quick Mini Sausage Wraps

Michelle Campen
Peoria, IL

So fast and easy to make when friends drop by.

3 10-oz. pkgs. mini smoked
    sausages

1 lb. bacon, sliced into thirds
1/2 c. brown sugar, packed

Wrap each cocktail wiener with a bacon piece; secure with a toothpick.
Arrange in an ungreased shallow baking pan; sprinkle generously with
brown sugar. Bake at 350 degrees until bacon is done, about
one hour; transfer to a serving plate. Makes 30 servings.

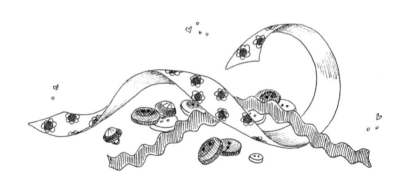

Marbles, toys, trinkets, beads or game pieces can
become a clever memory jar collage. Just use a
putty knife to apply a thick layer of premixed tile
cement to a small section of a lamp base or pottery
jar. Set the pieces into the cement; repeat until lamp
or jar is covered. Let air dry several days.

Lemonade with Strawberry Ice Cubes

Shelley Duffy
Winona, MN

So much better than store bought!

3 c. fresh lemon juice   4 c. cold water
2 c. sugar

Mix juice and sugar in a pitcher until sugar dissolves; add water. Place a couple of strawberry ice cubes in a glass; pour lemonade on top to fill. Makes 4 servings.

Strawberry Ice Cubes:

2 c. strawberries, hulled and   2 T. sugar
    sliced

Purée strawberries and sugar together in a blender; pour into an ice cube tray. Freeze.

Old-fashioned bed springs make fun candleholders...just slip a pillar candle inside!

Cinnamon & Ginger Treats

Debbie Isaacson
Irvine, CA

You won't be able to stop nibbling on these.

3 c. assorted nuts
1 egg white
1 T. orange juice
2/3 c. sugar

1 t. cinnamon
1/2 t. ground ginger
1/2 t. allspice
1/4 t. salt

Place nuts in a large mixing bowl; set aside. Blend egg white and orange juice together until frothy; mix in remaining ingredients. Pour over nuts; mix thoroughly. Spread coated nuts onto an aluminum foil-lined baking sheet; bake at 275 degrees for 45 minutes, stirring every 15 minutes. Cool; store in an airtight container. Makes 3 cups.

Pumpkin Dip

Vicky Couser
St. Paris, OH

A favorite recipe shared by my sister. To serve, spoon into a hollowed out pumpkin with lots of bite-size gingersnaps.

8-oz. pkg. cream cheese,
   softened
1/2 c. canned pumpkin

1/2 c. powdered sugar
1/2 c. brown sugar, packed
1-1/2 t. pumpkin pie spice

Blend cream cheese with pumpkin; mix in remaining ingredients. Add to a microwave-safe bowl; microwave on low until heated through without boiling. Whisk ingredients together while warm; serve immediately. Makes about 2-1/2 cups.

Hot & Spicy Cheese Dip

Patty Vance
Paulding, OH

One evening after a ceramics class, I found my car wouldn't start. While waiting for my husband to arrive, the class instructor took me upstairs to her kitchen and whipped up this tasty spread. Try spreading on onion crackers for a nice change.

2 lbs. pasteurized processed
   cheese spread, softened
1/2 c. plus 2 T. mayonnaise

5-oz. jar prepared horseradish,
   drained
10 to 12 drops hot pepper sauce

Blend all ingredients together; cover and refrigerate until chilled. Makes about 5 cups.

A collection of cross-stitched hand towels or table runners make the the prettiest valances when simply draped over a tension rod.

It's Snacktime!

Creamy Dijon-Ham Spread

Suzanne Novotny
Raeford, NC

Pretzels, veggies, crackers...this appetizer's terrific with anything!

8-oz. pkg. cream cheese,
   softened
2 T. mayonnaise
1 t. Dijon mustard

2/3 c. shredded Cheddar cheese
2 green onions, minced
3 slices cooked ham, finely
   chopped

Combine all ingredients; place in a serving crock. Cover and chill before serving. Makes about 3 cups.

Don't pass up a vintage kitchen chair or rocker at a tag sale. Freshen it up with a coat of paint then decoupage copies of handwritten recipe cards or pages from a children's book onto the chair seat or back...what a sweet shower gift.

Sparkling Raspberry Punch

Kathleen Kosinski
West Mifflin, PA

A sweet-tart combination that's so tasty.

46-oz. can pineapple juice
6-oz. can frozen pink lemonade
   concentrate, thawed
16-oz. container raspberry
   sherbet

2-ltr. bottle ginger ale, chilled
10-oz. pkg. frozen raspberries,
   thawed

Mix juices, sherbet and ginger ale in a large punch bowl; stir in undrained raspberries. Makes 4-1/2 quarts.

Tropical Smoothie

Natalie Taylor
Indian Wells, CA

Peel and chop mangoes, add to a plastic zipping bag and keep in the freezer...ready when you are!

1 c. orange juice
5 cubes frozen mango

2 to 3 frozen strawberries,
   hulled

Place all ingredients in a blender; blend until smooth, about 45 to 60 seconds. Serves one.

It's Snacktime!

Frozen Fruit Slush

Brenda Huey
Geneva, IN

*When the kids want something cool and refreshing,
I know this recipe will hit the spot.*

2 T. granulated sugar substitute
2 c. boiling water
12-oz. can frozen orange juice
    concentrate, partially thawed
16-oz. can crushed pineapple

16-oz. can fruit cocktail
16-oz. can diced peaches
11-oz. can mandarin oranges
7 bananas, peeled and sliced

Combine first 3 ingredients; set aside. Blend remaining ingredients together; add orange juice mixture. Pour into 8-ounce styrofoam cups; cover each with aluminum foil. Place in freezer; freeze. Remove from freezer 30 minutes before serving. Makes 22 to 24 servings.

Soft, faded scraps of velvet make the prettiest pincushions. Use pinking shears to cut several squares the same size, then stack them and stitch together across one side. Pins will be secured by just slipping through each layer.

Always-Requested Spinach Dip

Jennifer Clingan
Dayton, OH

Is there anyone who doesn't love this?

1 c. mayonnaise
2 c. sour cream
1.8-oz. pkg. leek soup mix or
   1-1/2 oz. pkg. onion
   soup mix
4-oz. can water chestnuts,
   drained and chopped

10-oz. pkg. frozen chopped
   spinach, thawed and drained
1-lb. loaf round pumpernickel
   bread

Combine first 5 ingredients, using only half the envelope if onion soup mix is used; mix well. Cover and refrigerate overnight. Slice off top of bread; gently tear out center, reserving bread for dipping. Spoon spinach mixture into the center of the bread; serve cold. Serves 8.

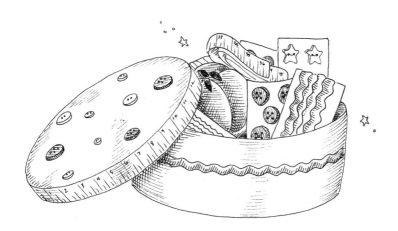

Be sure to pick up hatboxes whenever they can be found...terrific for corralling clutter!

It's Snacktime!

Parmesan Tomatoes

Irene Robinson
Cincinnati, OH

A tasty, old-fashioned dish...cut into wedges for easy snacking.

5 to 6 tomatoes
1/2 c. sour cream
1/2 c. mayonnaise
1/4 c. grated Parmesan cheese

1 t. garlic powder
juice of one lemon
1 t. fresh parsley, chopped
3 green onions, chopped

Slice tomatoes in half crosswise; set aside. Combine remaining ingredients; mound evenly on top of tomato halves. Broil until bubbly. Makes 10 to 12.

Stuffed Mushrooms

Jo Ann

Easy to make ahead...just chop, sauté, stuff and then cover with plastic wrap and refrigerate for up to 2 hours. Bake and serve when guests arrive.

20 mushrooms
1/4 c. onion, chopped
2 cloves garlic, minced
10-oz. pkg. frozen chopped
   spinach, thawed and drained
1 T. margarine

1/4 c. grated Parmesan cheese
1/4 c. bread crumbs
1/4 c. minced pimento
1/2 t. dried basil
1/2 t. dried oregano
salt and pepper to taste

Remove stems from mushrooms; set caps to side. Chop stems; sauté with onion and garlic in margarine until tender. Add spinach; heat on low until liquid is evaporated. Remove from heat; stir in remaining ingredients. Spoon into mushroom caps; arrange in a jelly-roll pan sprayed with non-stick vegetable spray. Bake at 425 degrees until golden, about 10 to 15 minutes; serve warm. Makes 20.

Cucumber Spread

Laura Fuller
Fort Wayne, IN

Refreshing with the zippy taste of lemon! Try this for a change-of-pace chip dip.

1 cucumber, peeled and diced
1 t. salt
8-oz. pkg. cream cheese,
    softened

2 T. sour cream
2 t. fresh thyme, chopped
1 t. lemon zest
1/4 t. pepper

Combine cucumber and salt in a food processor; purée. Strain mixture through a sieve into a medium mixing bowl; mix in remaining ingredients. Makes about 2 cups.

Garden-Fresh Veggie Dip

Angela Nichols
Mt. Airy, NC

Ready in a jiffy!

2/3 c. sour cream
1/3 c. mayonnaise
2 T. fresh chives, chopped
2 T. onion, minced

2 T. pimento, drained and
    chopped
1/2 t. garlic salt

Mix all ingredients together; chill. Makes about 1-1/2 cups.

Zesty Bacon Spread

Jennifer Gubbins
Homewood, IL

My dear Auntie Pammy shared this recipe with me years ago…still a family favorite year 'round. It makes plenty for a family get-together…just serve alongside tortilla chips.

16-oz. pkg. Mexican pasteurized
   processed cheese
   spread, cubed
2 8-oz. pkgs. cream cheese,
   softened
1/4 c. butter, softened

1/4 c. onion, minced
1 T. diced jalapeños
2 lbs. bacon, crisply cooked and
   crumbled

Cream cheeses and butter; blend in onion and jalapeños. Mix in bacon.
Makes about 5 cups.

Durable, yet in a variety of splashy colors and patterns, barkcloth draperies and slipcovers are at almost every auction or flea market. Snap them up for covering photo albums, hatboxes, luggage, lampshades, purses and pillows.

7-Layer Dip

Renee Henry
Mount Vernon, OH

Try something new for dipping...cut corn tortillas into wedges, sprinkle to taste with lime juice, chili powder and salt then bake at 350 degrees for 5 minutes. Terrific!

16-oz. can refried beans
2 c. sour cream
1-1/4 oz. pkg. taco seasoning
   mix
2 avocados, peeled and mashed
2 t. lemon juice

3 cloves garlic, minced
2 c. shredded Colby Jack cheese
4 green onions, diced
1/4 c. black olives, sliced
1 tomato, diced

Spread beans in the bottom of a 10" pie pan; set aside. Combine sour cream and taco seasoning mix; spread over beans. Mix avocados, lemon juice and garlic together; layer over sour cream mixture. Sprinkle with cheese; top with onions, olives and tomatoes. Serves 8.

A collection of vintage laundry bags will brighten any utility room...as practical and pretty now as they were then.

It's Snacktime!

Dilly Dip

Melody Hunter
Butler, PA

Veggies are great, but for a change, try spreading this on thick slices of sourdough or pumpernickel bread.

1 T. dill weed
2 t. dried chives
2 t. dried, minced onion

1 c. mayonnaise
1 c. sour cream
salt and pepper to taste

Mix all ingredients together; cover and chill for 2 hours. Makes 2 cups.

A Toast for Any Occasion

Connie Hilty
Pearland, TX

Use cookie cutters to cut the toast into fun shapes that go along with the occasion for an extra-special touch.

15-oz. loaf bread, crusts
    trimmed
1/2 c. butter, melted
1/2 t. curry powder

1/2 t. turmeric
1/2 t. ground cumin
1/2 t. salt
1/4 t. paprika

Slice bread into 1/2-inch thick slices; arrange on an ungreased baking sheet. Set aside. Whisk remaining ingredients together in a small bowl; spread over both sides of bread slices. Bake at 400 degrees for 4 minutes; turn slices over and bake until crisp, about 3 additional minutes. Makes about 2 dozen.

Veggie Roll-Ups

Sherri Garee
Newark, OH

*Add some fun...use colorful toothpick frills to secure
each individual serving.*

2 8-oz. pkgs. cream cheese,
  softened
1-oz. pkg. ranch dip mix
2 T. milk
1/2 c. sour cream

1/2 c. shredded Cheddar cheese
1 c. assorted vegetables,
  chopped
10-1/2 oz. pkg. flour tortillas

Mix cream cheese, dip mix, milk, sour cream, cheese and vegetables
together; spread over tortillas. Roll up and place seam-side down in a
shallow baking pan; refrigerate until firm, at least 3 hours; cut each
into fourths and arrange on a serving plate. Serves 8 to 10.

*Fill antique decanters with lotions or liquid soaps...
so much nicer than plastic bottles.*

It's Snacktime!

Cheese Straws

Judy Borecky
Escondido, CA

These are addictive!

2 c. all-purpose flour
2 c. shredded Cheddar cheese
1 t. baking powder

1/2 t. salt
6 T. ice water
1 c. margarine, softened

Combine all ingredients; chill. Roll out to 1/4-inch thickness; cut into 2"x1/2" pieces. Arrange on ungreased baking sheets; bake at 350 degrees for 10 to 12 minutes. Serves 4.

Italian Eggplant Sticks

Karen Pilcher
Burleson, TX

Serve with lots of salsa, sour cream and warm marinara sauce.

3 eggplant, peeled
1 c. Italian seasoned
   bread crumbs
1 t. salt

1 t. pepper
3 eggs
1/4 c. milk
oil for deep frying

Cut eggplant into 3"x1/2" sticks; place in ice water for 30 minutes. Drain; set aside. Combine bread crumbs, salt and pepper; set aside. Blend eggs and milk together in a shallow bowl; dip in eggplant sticks. Coat sticks with bread crumbs; arrange on a baking sheet. Cover; chill for 30 minutes. Heat one-inch depth oil in a deep skillet; add eggplant sticks. Heat until golden on both sides, about 2 minutes. Remove to drain on paper towels. Serves 6.

Hot Pepperoni Dip

Vickie

For a milder version, use banana peppers. Keep lots of toasted bread sticks or garlic bread on hand for dipping...yum!

2 c. shredded mozzarella cheese
2 c. shredded sharp Cheddar
   cheese
2 c. mayonnaise
1 red onion, chopped

4-oz. can diced green chiles,
   drained
2 to 3 jalapeño peppers
10 to 20 pepperoni slices

Combine cheeses, mayonnaise, onion, chiles and peppers; place in an ungreased 13"x9" baking pan. Layer pepperoni on top; bake at 350 degrees for 45 minutes. Serves 10.

Creamy Mushroom Spread

Marybeth Kusner
Swarthmore, PA

To keep the dip warm, spoon into a fondue pot or mini slow cooker. Serve with thick slices of crusty French bread.

10-3/4 oz. can cream of
   mushroom soup with garlic
8-oz. pkg. cream cheese,
   softened

2-1/2 oz. pkg. pepperoni,
   chopped

Combine all ingredients; bake at 350 degrees until bubbly. Serves 6.

It's Snacktime!

Baja Bites

Pam Lewis
Munster, IN

Tasty tidbits!

5 eggs, beaten
1 c. cottage cheese
1/4 c. all-purpose flour
1/2 t. baking powder
1/4 c. butter, melted

2 T. green onion, minced
4-oz. can green chiles, drained
2 c. shredded Monterey Jack
   cheese

Combine eggs and cottage cheese; blend until almost smooth. Add flour, baking powder and butter; stir in onion, chiles and cheese. Pour into a lightly greased 8"x8" baking pan; bake at 350 degrees for 30 to 40 minutes. Let cool slightly; cut into squares. Serves 8.

With the help of a color copier, it's easy to turn vintage cookbook covers into a pretty kitchen border! Just coat the wall and back of each copy using a foam brush and matte finish decoupage medium. Position on wall, smooth edges and top with a thin layer of decoupage medium to seal.

Pecan-Wrapped Blue Cheese Ball

Sandra Carron
Raymond, IL

Our whole family loves blue cheese and this is one of our favorite ways to enjoy it.

2 8-oz. pkgs. cream cheese,
   softened
2 c. shredded Cheddar cheese
1/2 c. butter, softened
2 T. Worcestershire sauce

1-1/2 t. garlic powder
4 to 6-oz. pkg. crumbled blue
   cheese
1 to 2 T. dried, minced onion
crushed pecans

Mix all ingredients, except the pecans, together; divide in half. Shape each into a ball; roll in pecans. Wrap in plastic wrap and chill until firm. Serves 8 to 10.

Have some fun! A whimsical vintage child's sand pail can hold anything from toothbrushes to pens and pencils.

Hot & hearty... Soup's On!

Cream of Tomato Soup

Mari Vandersloot
Havre, MT

A big steaming bowl alongside everyone's favorite, a grilled cheese sandwich, and you've got a fantastic lunch or dinner!

32-oz. can diced tomatoes
9-oz. can chicken broth
1 T. butter
2 T. sugar

1 T. onion, chopped
1/8 t. baking soda
2 c. whipping cream
Optional: shredded cheese

Mix tomatoes, broth, butter, sugar, onions and baking soda in a stockpot; simmer for one hour, stirring occasionally. Gradually add cream; heat until warmed through, stirring constantly. Garnish with a sprinkle of cheese, if desired. Serves 4.

Have fun flea marketing...feel like turning a garden bench into a coffee table? Go right ahead!

Chicken Pot-Pie Soup

Jennifer Clingan
Dayton, OH

*I love to make this soup on chilly days...it warms me head-to-toe.
Although it does take a little extra time to prepare, the results
are well worth it.*

1-1/2 c. butter
1-1/2 c. all-purpose flour
4 t. salt
1/2 t. pepper
4 c. half-and-half
6 c. seasoned chicken broth

6 boneless, skinless chicken
  breasts, cooked and cubed
5 to 6 potatoes, cubed and
  boiled
3 c. mixed vegetables

Melt butter in a large Dutch oven; whisk in flour, salt and pepper.
Heat and stir over low heat until smooth and bubbly; remove from
heat. Carefully whisk in half-and-half and broth; return to heat and
bring to a slow boil. Reduce heat; add remaining ingredients, chopping
into bite-size pieces if necessary. Simmer until vegetables are tender.
Makes 8 to 10 servings.

Spot a steel lawn chair? Grab it! Those slightly springy chairs from the 1940's are just as comfy today and can be revived with a little enamel paint.

Rich & Meaty Chili

Sarah Cline
Las Vegas, NV

Don't forget all the good things that go with this...hearty crackers, golden cornbread or thick slices of homebaked bread. Yum!

1 lb. ground beef
1/2 c. onion, chopped
2 T. butter
2 15-1/2 oz. cans kidney beans
2 15-oz. cans chili beans
4 c. tomatoes, diced
6-oz. can tomato paste
2 to 3 t. chili powder
1-1/2 t. salt
1/2 t. dried oregano
1/4 t. pepper
1/8 t. hot pepper sauce
1 bay leaf
1-1/2 c. water
1 c. celery, chopped
1 c. green pepper, chopped
Garnish: shredded Cheddar
        cheese and sour cream

Brown ground beef with onion; drain. Place into a Dutch oven; stir in remaining ingredients. Bring to a boil; reduce heat and simmer for one hour. Cover and simmer for 10 minutes; remove bay leaf before serving. Spoon into serving bowls; garnish with cheese and sour cream. Serves 6 to 8.

Vintage shop signs are always in style hanging in a gathering room, kitchen or on the porch.

Creamy Potato-Ham Soup

Jane Murray
APO, AE

Have bowls of favorite toppings ready...scallions, Cheddar cheese, sour cream, croutons and oyster crackers.

3 potatoes, peeled and cubed
1 onion, chopped
1 c. water
1 c. ham or Canadian bacon
    chopped
3 c. milk

1 to 2 c. instant mashed potato
    flakes
1 T. fresh parsley, chopped
1 t. salt
1-1/2 t. white pepper

Heat first 3 ingredients in a Dutch oven until potatoes are tender; stir in ham or Canadian bacon and milk, heating through. Add potato flakes for desired thickness; stir in parsley, salt and pepper. Serves 6.

Remember the old-time soda pop thermometers? They'd look great on the garden shed!

Hot & hearty... Soup's On!

Cheesy Corn Chowder

Melissa Huston
Bangor, ME

Spoon servings into retro enamelware mugs...just for fun!

1 onion, chopped
1 clove garlic, minced
1 T. butter
2 potatoes, peeled and cubed
15-1/4 oz. can corn, drained
14-3/4 oz. can creamed corn

10-3/4 oz. can Cheddar cheese
    soup
2 c. milk
1 c. shredded Cheddar cheese
cayenne pepper and salt to taste

Sauté onion and garlic in butter in a heavy stockpot until tender; add potatoes and just enough water to cover. Bring to a boil; reduce heat and simmer for 10 minutes. Add remaining ingredients; heat over low heat until potatoes are tender, about 10 to 15 additional minutes, stirring constantly. Makes 4 servings.

Roomy graniteware dishpans are the perfect size for filling with ice to keep bottles of pop cool and frosty at any outdoor get-together.

Chicken & Wild Rice Soup

Julia List
Lincoln, NE

A thoughtful friend always brought our family this after the birth of each of our children. We loved it so much that finally, after my third child, I asked for the recipe!

2 c. cooked chicken, diced
6-oz. box long-grain wild rice, cooked
2 10-3/4 oz. cans cream of mushroom soup
10-3/4 oz. can cream of celery soup

14-1/2 oz. can chicken broth
Optional: 2 T. sherry
1 carrot, shredded
4-oz. pkg. sliced mushrooms
1 pt. half-and-half

Combine all ingredients except half-and-half in a large stockpot; heat until vegetables are tender. Reduce heat to low; gradually stir in half-and-half, heating thoroughly without boiling, about 30 minutes. Stir often. Serves 6.

Give any table setting a splash of color! Be sure to snap up colorful glasses called "Fiesta® go-alongs" whenever they're spotted. Their bright colors and Mexican motifs can't be missed.

French Onion Soup

Kristine Marumoto
Sandy, UT

A classic soup that's really easy to make.

6 onions, thinly sliced
1 T. oil
4 T. butter, divided
6 c. beef broth
salt and pepper to taste
1/2 c. Gruyère cheese, shredded
   and divided

1/2 c. shredded Swiss cheese,
   divided
1/2 c. grated Parmesan cheese,
   divided
6 slices French bread, toasted

Heat onion in oil and 2 tablespoons butter over low heat in a 3-quart saucepan until tender; add broth. Bring to a boil; reduce heat and simmer for 30 minutes. Remove from heat; season with salt and pepper. Ladle equally into 6 oven-safe serving bowls; sprinkle each bowl with equal amounts of each cheese. Arrange one bread slice on top of cheeses. Melt remaining butter; drizzle over bread slices. Place bowls on a baking sheet; bake at 425 degrees for 10 minutes. Broil until cheeses are golden; serve immediately. Makes 6 servings.

Novelty tablecloths are always a popular flea market classic. They make terrific gifts for birthdays, bridal showers and housewarmings...not to mention, keeping one for yourself too!

Rainbow Pasta Salad

Sandy Lynch
Iroquois, SD

Add any of your favorite vegetables...the result is a terrific salad!

6-oz. can whole pitted black
   olives
1 pt. cherry tomatoes
1 onion, diced
1 green pepper, diced

10-1/2 oz. pkg. rainbow rotini,
   cooked and cooled
16-oz. bottle Italian dressing
Garnish: grated Parmesan
   cheese

Mix all ingredients together; cover and refrigerate overnight. Sprinkle
with Parmesan cheese before serving. Serves 8 to 10.

*Try slipping rose blossoms into old-fashioned egg
cups...charming at each place setting.*

The Best-Ever Potato Salad

Shellye McDaniel
Texarkana, TX

A homestyle potato salad that's just plain good!

4 c. potatoes, peeled, cubed and
   boiled
1 c. mayonnaise
4 hard-boiled eggs, peeled and
   chopped
1-1/2 c. celery, chopped
1/4 c. radishes, chopped

1/2 c. green onions, chopped
1-1/2 t. salt
1/2 t. celery seed
1 T. cider vinegar
2 t. mustard
2 T. fresh parsley, chopped
1 t. pepper

Combine ingredients in a large serving bowl; mix well. Cover and refrigerate until serving. Serves 6 to 8.

If you're looking at linens and they're a bit yellow with age, don't pass them up. Brighten them with a soaking in cool water mixed with white vinegar. For stubborn stains, dab some lemon juice on the spot and lay the piece in the sun to dry.

Spinach Salad with Strawberries

Michele Olson
Safety Harbor, FL

Looks so elegant, but it's a snap to make.

2 bunches spinach, rinsed and
    torn
1 pt. strawberries, hulled and
    sliced
1/2 c. sugar
2 T. sesame seed

1 T. poppy seed
1-1/2 t. onion, minced
1/4 t. Worcestershire sauce
1/4 t. paprika
1/2 c. oil
1/4 c. cider vinegar

Toss spinach and strawberries together in a serving bowl; set aside.
Add the next 7 ingredients to a blender; gradually add vinegar,
blending until thickened. Pour over salad before serving. Serves 8.

*Fat wire clam baskets make great hearthside
kindling holders, or set one in the mudroom to
collect the kids' rain boots.*

Marinated Cucumber Salad

Jordan Baker
Fountain, NC

I think this is the best for summertime suppers or church picnics.

2 cucumbers, thinly sliced
1 onion, sliced into rings
2 c. carrots, sliced
1/2 c. celery, chopped
1 c. white wine vinegar

1/4 c. oil
3/4 c. sugar
1 t. celery seed
1 t. salt
1 t. pepper

Combine cucumbers, onion, carrots and celery; set aside. Whisk remaining ingredients together; pour over vegetables. Cover; chill for 8 to 10 hours. Serves 4.

Crunchy Cauliflower Salad

Laurie Steller
Bigfork, MT

Saves time...you make it the night before.

1 head lettuce, torn
1 head cauliflower, chopped
1 sweet onion, chopped
1 lb. bacon, crisply cooked and
  crumbled

1/2 c. sugar
1/3 c. grated Parmesan cheese
salt and pepper to taste
2 c. mayonnaise

In a large bowl, combine lettuce, cauliflower, onion and bacon; toss well. Set aside. Mix together sugar and Parmesan cheese; sprinkle over lettuce mixture; salt and pepper to taste. Spread mayonnaise on top; cover and refrigerate overnight. Toss gently before serving. Serves 8.

No-Peek Stew

Mary Jo Urbaniak
Spokane, WA

The hard part is not peeking!

2-1/2 lbs. stew beef
2 onions, quartered
4 stalks celery, chopped
4 potatoes, peeled and cubed
3 carrots, sliced
2 t. tapioca

1 T. sugar
salt and pepper to taste
10-3/4 oz. can tomato soup
1-1/4 c. water
10-oz. pkg. frozen peas

Add ingredients in order listed to a Dutch oven; cover. Bake at 325 degrees for 4 hours. Serves 4.

Tomato-Beef Stew

Carol Fulton
Idaho Falls, ID

The blend of herbs and spices in the steak sauce
creates a rich, delicious stew.

4 carrots, sliced
2 stalks celery, sliced
4 potatoes, diced
1 onion, diced

1-1/2 lbs. ground beef, browned
16-oz. can stewed tomatoes
1/2 to 1 c. red steak sauce

Place carrots, celery, potatoes and onion in a stockpot; cover with water. Boil until tender; drain. Stir in ground beef and tomatoes; add steak sauce to taste. Heat through. Serves 4 to 6.

Chicken & Dumplings

Amy Weigel
Las Vegas, NV

*There's just something about chicken & dumplings
that makes it an all-time comfort food.*

2 boneless, skinless chicken
    breasts, cut into strips
1/8 t. salt
1/8 t. pepper
1 T. olive oil
2 T. all-purpose flour
14-1/2 oz. can chicken broth
1 c. water

1 onion, sliced
1 c. green beans
1 c. carrots, shredded
2/3 c. biscuit baking mix
1/3 c. cornmeal
1/4 c. shredded Cheddar cheese
1/2 c. milk

Season chicken with salt and pepper; brown in a skillet with oil.
Sprinkle flour over the top; stir in broth, water, onions, beans and
carrots. Bring to a boil; reduce heat and simmer for 5 minutes. In
another bowl, combine baking mix, cornmeal and cheese; stir in milk.
Drop by tablespoonfuls into soup; return to a boil. Simmer, covered,
for 10 to 12 minutes. Serves 4.

*Could that secondhand dresser become a vanity
for a sink in the new bathroom? Sure! Instead of
buying a brand new vanity, recycle
something from the past.*

Old-Fashioned Pea Salad

Angela Manus
Huntsville, AL

A familiar favorite that everyone will love!

16-oz. pkg. frozen peas, blanched
1-3/4 c. mild Cheddar cheese, diced
3 hard-boiled eggs, peeled and diced

1/2 c. celery, diced
1/8 c. green pepper, diced
1 T. diced pimento
1-1/2 T. onion, minced
salt and pepper to taste
2 to 4 T. mayonnaise

Gently combine all ingredients; cover and chill until serving. Makes 4 to 6 servings.

Vintage postage stamps and stickers can be decoupaged onto lampshades, pails, tin picnic baskets or picture frames...so easy!

Snap Salad

Sylvia Schutt
Burkeville, VA

Why the funny name? Because it's ready in a snap!

2 1-qt. jars green beans,
 drained
1/2 c. onion, chopped
2/3 c. oil
1/2 c. vinegar

1/2 t. salt
1/4 t. pepper
5 slices bacon, crisply cooked
 and crumbled
lettuce leaves

Combine first 6 ingredients together; cover and chill overnight. Drain well; mix in bacon. Line a serving bowl with lettuce leaves; fill with green bean mixture. Form a well in the center; fill with dressing. Serves 12.

Dressing:

5 hard-boiled eggs, peeled and
 chopped
1/3 c. mayonnaise

1 t. mustard
2 t. vinegar
1/2 t. salt

Stir ingredients together.

Remnants of soft and cuddly chenille bedspreads can get new life when used to reupholster a toddler's chair. So sweet!

Texas Ranch Soup

Deborah Neuman
San Felipe, TX

So good, this may only make 2 Texas-size servings!

1-1/2 lbs. ground beef, browned
2 15-oz. cans ranch-style beans
2 15-oz. cans corn
2 14-1/2 oz. cans diced
  tomatoes

1-1/4 oz. pkg. taco seasoning
  mix
Garnish: crushed tortilla chips
  and shredded Cheddar
  cheese

Combine ingredients in a large stockpot; bring to a boil. Reduce heat and simmer for 15 minutes. Spoon into serving bowls; garnish with crushed tortilla chips and shredded Cheddar cheese. Serves 6.

Cajun Corn Soup

Marie Stahl
Frankfort, IN

*Before serving, sprinkle with more cayenne if you want
a Cajun soup with kick!*

4 c. water
6-oz. can tomato paste
1 t. salt
1 t. pepper
1/2 t. cayenne pepper
1 green pepper, chopped

1 red pepper, chopped
2 c. frozen corn
1/2 onion, chopped
4 cloves garlic, minced
1 T. oil
1/2 lb. ground beef

Combine the first 8 ingredients in a large stockpot; heat over high heat to a boil. Reduce heat; simmer for 35 minutes. Sauté onion and garlic in oil in a 12" skillet until tender; add to soup. Brown ground beef in same skillet; drain. Stir into soup; simmer 10 additional minutes. Serves 6 to 8.

Hot & hearty... Soup's On!

Italian Vegetable Soup

Janet Allen
Hauser, ID

Fill an old-fashioned canning jar with this soup and deliver to a friend who's feeling under the weather...she'll love it.

1 lb. ground beef, browned
1 c. onions, diced
1 c. celery, chopped
1 c. carrots, sliced
2 cloves garlic, minced
16-oz. can tomatoes
15-oz. can tomato sauce
15-oz. can kidney beans
3 c. water
5 t. beef bouillon granules

1 T. dried parsley
1 t. salt
1/2 t. dried oregano
1/2 t. dried basil
1/4 t. pepper
2 c. cabbage, shredded
1/2 c. elbow macaroni, uncooked
Garnish: grated Parmesan
          cheese

Combine the first 15 ingredients in a stockpot; bring to a boil. Lower heat; simmer for 20 minutes. Add cabbage and macaroni; bring to a boil. Reduce heat and simmer until vegetables are tender; sprinkle with Parmesan cheese before serving. Makes 10 servings.

Slide an old porcelain tray behind the kitchen sink faucets...a terrific backsplash!

77

Classic Broccoli Salad

Karen Chandler
Madison Heights, MI

So versatile! Substitute a head of chopped cauliflower for one of the heads of broccoli, or toss in some cashews or chow mein noodles for extra crunch!

2 heads broccoli, chopped
1 lb. bacon, crisply cooked and
   crumbled
1/2 c. sunflower seeds
1/2 c. golden raisins
1 red onion, diced
2 c. shredded Cheddar cheese
1 c. mayonnaise
2 T. vinegar
1/8 c. sugar

Toss first 5 ingredients together in a serving bowl; set aside. Mix remaining ingredients together in a small mixing bowl; pour over broccoli mixture, tossing until well coated. Cover and refrigerate until serving. Serves 8 to 10.

Falling in love with a handmade quilt or tablecloth that's stained? Turn the best parts into pillowcases...that's the fun of it all!

Family Reunion Salad

Jackie Balla
Walbridge, OH

Feeds a crowd!

2 3-oz. pkgs. Oriental ramen
  noodles
1 T. butter
1-1/2 c. Italian Parmesan-
  flavored sliced almonds
2 c. Colby Jack cheese, cubed

2 apples, cored, peeled and diced
2 10-oz. pkgs. romaine lettuce,
  torn
1 lb. bacon, crisply cooked and
  crumbled

Sauté noodles in butter until golden; place in a large serving bowl.
Gently toss in remaining ingredients; pour dressing on top before
serving. Serves 12.

Dressing:

1/3 c. sugar
3/4 c. oil
1/2 c. white vinegar

2 seasoning packets from ramen
  noodles
5 drops soy sauce

Whisk ingredients together.

Blanket chests or trunks can do double-duty as coffee tables and storage spots for coasters, videos or remote controls.

Strawberry-Rhubarb Salad

Jeanette Martin
Homer, AK

A favorite pie combination is terrific as a salad too!

3 c. rhubarb, chopped
1/2 c. sugar
1/4 t. salt
3 c. water, divided
2 3-oz. pkgs. strawberry gelatin
   mix

1 c. celery, chopped
1 T. lemon juice
1/2 c. chopped nuts

Place rhubarb, sugar, salt and 1/4 cup water in a saucepan; heat until rhubarb is tender. Add gelatin mix, celery, lemon juice, nuts and remaining water; stir well. Pour into a mold or 8"x8" glass dish; refrigerate until firm. Serves 8.

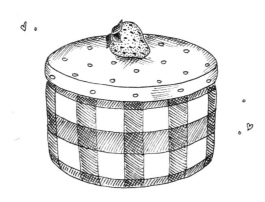

Because it's so roomy, try setting a weathered wheelbarrow next to the sofa to hold books and magazines. The bonus? It can be easily moved from room to room.

Glistening Strawberry Salad

Jean Stokes
Ozark, AL

Makes such a pretty presentation.

6-oz. pkg. strawberry gelatin
   mix
1-1/2 c. boiling water

10-oz. pkg. frozen sweetened
   strawberries, thawed
8-oz. can crushed pineapple
1 c. sour cream

Dissolve gelatin mix in water in a medium mixing bowl; add strawberries and pineapple. Strain mixture; return fruit to mixing bowl. Set aside one cup of the juice. Pour fruit mixture and remaining juice into a 5-cup mold or 9" square baking pan that's been lightly coated with non-stick vegetable spray. Cover and refrigerate for one hour or until set. Whisk sour cream with reserved juice; pour over fruit mixture. Cover; refrigerate until set. Cut into squares. Serves 8.

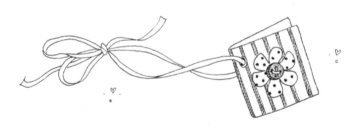

Fresh Cranberry Salad

Marion Pfeifer
Smyrna, DE

This salad is always on our Christmas Day buffet table.

6-oz. pkg. lemon gelatin mix
1/2 c. sugar
2 c. boiling water
20-oz. can crushed pineapple

1 lb. cranberries, ground
1 c. celery, diced
3/4 c. chopped pecans

Dissolve gelatin mix and sugar in water; add remaining ingredients. Mix well; pour into a 5-cup mold. Chill until firm, about 4 hours. Serves 8.

Homestyle Kale Soup

Tracy Melancon
APO, AE

Warm and filling for a family on the go.

4 10-1/2 oz. cans chicken broth
4 10-1/2 oz. cans beef broth
8 c. kale, shredded
3 potatoes, peeled and cubed
1 onion, chopped
3 carrots, sliced

2 stalks celery, chopped
1 T. oil
14-1/2 oz. can tomatoes
1-1/2 lbs. Kielbasa, sliced
16-oz. can pinto beans
hot pepper sauce to taste

Pour first 4 ingredients into a large stockpot; heat over medium heat until potatoes are tender. Sauté onions, carrots and celery in oil until tender; add to broth mixture. Stir in tomatoes and Kielbasa; simmer for 30 minutes. Add beans; season with hot pepper sauce. Simmer until thoroughly heated through. Serves 10.

Need a little more organization on your desk? Use an apothecary chest. Its many drawers hold pens, pencils, rubber bands and paper clips in style.

Don't Forget to Eat Your Veggies

Partially visible handwritten recipe cards surround the central illustration:

(top left, partial) *...lloped Potatoes* / *Delinda Blakney* / *...sley, 1 t. sp...* / *..., 1 t. salt* / *f the po...* / *...rt cassero...* / *...p with 1/2...* / *...yers, spr...*

(right, partial) *...kin' Zucch...* / *2 eggs (sly...* / *2 c. (2 mea...* / *shredded u...* / *tbls. butter o...* / *pper. Stir u...* / *d in zucc...* / *...m heat. Th...*

Old-Fashioned Baked Corn

cans corn, drained

T. sugar

T. butter, melted

all-purpose flour

4 eggs, beaten

1/2 c. milk

8 oz. pkg. pasteurized processed cheese spread-cubed

Combine all ingredients together in a large mixing bowl; spread in an ungreased 2-qt. dish. Bake at 325° for 45 min.

Mom's Broccoli Casserole

Heather Alexander
Lacey, WA

Our holidays wouldn't be complete without this dish!

2 10-oz. pkgs. broccoli
2 T. onion, minced
5 T. butter, divided
3 T. all-purpose flour
1-1/2 c. milk
2 t. salt

1/4 t. pepper
3 hard-boiled eggs, peeled and
  chopped
1/2 c. shredded Cheddar cheese
1/2 c. corn flake cereal, crushed

Prepare broccoli as directed on package; set aside. Sauté onion in
3 tablespoons butter until tender; stir in flour. Add milk, salt and
pepper; bring to a boil, stirring often. Remove from heat; set aside.
Place broccoli in a greased 13"x9" baking pan; sprinkle with eggs.
Pour milk mixture over the top; stir well and set aside. Melt remaining
butter; combine with cheese and cereal. Crumble over broccoli mixture;
bake at 375 degrees for 20 minutes. Serves 8.

An old wooden artist's case makes a great choice for storing favorite keepsakes. Little nooks & crannies designed to hold painting supplies are ideal for postcards, seashells and other special treasures.

Family Gathering Potatoes

Andrea Bailey
Spencer, WV

Cheesy, creamy, yummy! Everyone will want seconds.

30-oz. pkg. frozen shredded
  hashbrowns
10-3/4 oz. can cream of chicken
  soup
1 onion, chopped

1/2 c. mushrooms, chopped
2 c. sour cream
2 c. shredded Cheddar cheese
1/2 c. potato chips, crushed
2 to 4 T. butter, melted

Mix hashbrowns, soup, onion, mushrooms and sour cream together; spread in a greased 13"x9" baking pan. Top with cheese; sprinkle with chips. Drizzle butter over top; bake at 350 degrees for 45 minutes to one hour, covering with aluminum foil if chips begin to brown. Serves 8.

Architectural pieces salvaged from old houses are terrific for perking up a garden shed. A wooden screen door easily becomes a trellis and pretty gingerbread trim dresses up a plain door or window in no time!

Sweet Potato Crunch

Theresa Fussell
Thibodaux, LA

Sprinkle some chopped pecans on top if you like extra crunch.

1/2 c. sugar
1 c. margarine, melted and
   divided
2 eggs, beaten
1 t. vanilla extract

1/2 c. milk
3 c. sweet potatoes, peeled,
   boiled and mashed
1 c. brown sugar, packed
1/2 c. all-purpose flour

Whisk sugar, 1/2 cup margarine, eggs, vanilla and milk together in a
large mixing bowl; blend in sweet potatoes. Spoon into a buttered
13"x9" baking pan; set aside. Combine brown sugar, flour and
remaining butter together; sprinkle over potato mixture. Bake at
350 degrees for 25 minutes. Serves 4.

Enamelware is often cast off if it has a rusty hole
in the bottom. But before tossing those colorful
pieces, give them a new life! Filled with potting soil
and colorful summertime blooms, they bring a touch
of whimsy to any porch.

Spoonbread

Cha McCarl
Enid, OK

A yummy Southern-style cornbread recipe.

2 eggs, beaten
8-1/2 oz. pkg. corn muffin mix
12-oz. can creamed corn
12-oz. can corn, drained

1/4 c. margarine, melted
1 c. sour cream
1 c. shredded Cheddar cheese

Combine the first 6 ingredients; stir well. Spread into a lightly buttered 11"x7" baking pan; bake at 350 degrees for 35 minutes. Sprinkle cheese on top; return to oven until melted. Serves 6.

Snap up wire baskets for a fresh twist on traditional windowboxes...use them inside or out!

Cabbage Rolls

Kim Berticio
Wallingford, CT

A favorite family reunion side.

1 head cabbage
2 lbs. ground beef
2 eggs
1 T. dried, minced onion
1/2 c. instant rice, uncooked

4 10-3/4 oz. cans tomato soup
10-3/4 oz. can cream of
    mushroom soup
2/3 c. catsup
salt and pepper to taste

Parboil cabbage; remove from heat and separate leaves, discarding core. Set aside. Combine ground beef, eggs, onion and rice; divide and spoon evenly down the centers of 12 cabbage leaves. Roll each up; set aside. Add soups and catsup to a stockpot; bring to a boil. Gently add cabbage rolls; salt and pepper to taste. Reduce heat and simmer for 2 to 2-1/2 hours, occasionally stirring gently. Makes 12 servings.

To give a newer piece of furniture a vintage look, try this tip before painting. Rub the corners and raised areas, where natural wear would occur, with candle wax. Candle wax resists paint making it easier to remove in those areas...just paint, let dry and lightly sand off paint where the wax was placed. So simple!

Don't forget to eat Your Veggies

Creamy Potatoes & Baby Peas

Sherry Satterwhite
Rogerson, ID

In Idaho there's always a lot of ways to use potatoes. Try this with tender new potatoes right out of the garden.

2-1/2 c. new redskin potatoes, cubed
1/2 c. baby green peas
2 T. all-purpose flour
2 c. milk, divided
2 T. butter
salt and pepper to taste

Place potatoes in a stockpot; cover with water. Boil until potatoes are tender, adding peas during last 4 minutes of cooking time; remove from heat. Drain; set aside. Whisk flour and 1/4 cup milk together until thickened; set aside. Pour remaining milk over potatoes and peas in the stockpot; add butter. Heat through; stir in flour mixture. Continue heating until warmed through and creamy. Salt and pepper to taste before serving. Serves 4.

For a new idea, try using vintage flower frogs to hold placecards.

Mom's Patio Beans

Karen Brothersen
Kemmerer, WY

No cookout would be the same without this side dish!

1 lb. ground beef
1 onion, chopped
salt and pepper to taste
10-3/4 oz. can tomato and rice
   soup

10-3/4 oz. can tomato soup
2 15-1/2 oz. cans kidney beans
1/2 c. brown sugar, packed
1 T. mustard

Brown beef with onion, salt and pepper in a 12" skillet; add remaining ingredients, mixing well. Spoon into an ungreased 13"x9" baking pan. Bake at 350 degrees until bubbly, about 45 minutes. Serves 6.

Create a simple centerpiece by tucking delicate Queen Anne's lace into retro tumblers filled with sea glass...so pretty on a summer picnic table.

Party Baked Beans

Kathleen Smith
Greensboro, NC

Just sit back and wait for the compliments!

2 28-oz. cans pork & beans
1/2 t. dry mustard
1 c. molasses
1 c. catsup
1 onion, chopped

2 green peppers, sliced
1/2 lb. Kielbasa, sliced
1/2 lb. bacon, diced
2 t. Worcestershire sauce

Combine all ingredients in a lightly buttered 13"x9" baking pan; bake at 325 degrees for 2 hours. Serves 6 to 8.

Creamy Coleslaw

Rebecca Fincher
Columbia, SC

Try adding some shredded carrots or red cabbage for more color.

1 c. sour cream
1/2 c. mayonnaise
2 t. celery seed
2 t. lemon juice

2 t. sugar
1 t. salt
1/2 t. white pepper
8 c. shredded cabbage

Combine sour cream, mayonnaise, celery seed, lemon juice, sugar, salt and pepper; mix well. Pour over cabbage; toss to coat. Cover and refrigerate until chilled. Serves 12.

Copper Pennies

Marie Thompson
Scottsville, VA

Make this recipe the night before for an easy do-ahead side.

2 lbs. carrots, sliced into
   1/4-inch slices
2 onions, sliced
1 green pepper, thinly sliced
10-3/4 oz. can tomato soup

2/3 c. sugar
1 t. Worcestershire sauce
1/2 c. oil
1/2 t. salt

Place carrot slices in a saucepan; cover with water. Bring to a boil; boil until carrots are tender, about 8 to 10 minutes. Drain; pour into a large serving bowl. Add onions and green pepper; toss gently. Whisk remaining ingredients together; pour over vegetable mixture, stirring to mix. Cover and refrigerate overnight. Serves 6 to 8.

Turn glass telephone-line insulators into votive holders...they're just the right size!

English Potato Cakes

Sandra Logston
New Martinsville, WV

*An old-fashioned recipe brought from England by the colonists,
updated and still enjoyed by all!*

2 potatoes, grated
2 eggs, beaten
1/2 c. all-purpose flour

1 t. baking powder
1/4 t. baking soda
1/4 t. salt

Combine potatoes and eggs; set aside. Stir flour, baking powder,
baking soda and salt together; add potato mixture, mixing well. Drop
on a hot skillet, one tablespoonful at a time, spreading with the back
of a wooden spoon; heat until set. Flip and heat until golden on both
sides. Serves 2 to 4.

A discarded footboard makes a clever wall
organizer! Add cup hooks to hold keys and a
salvaged slate chalkboard for jotting down
grocery and other "to-do" lists.

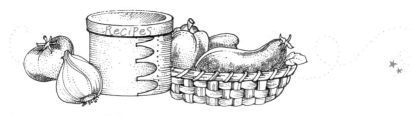

Garden Vegetable Pie

Wanda Kozlowski
Silver Creek, NY

Try serving wedges of this with chicken or
pork chops...everyone will ask for seconds!

2 c. prepared rice
1 egg, beaten
1/4 c. grated Parmesan cheese
1/4 c. fresh parsley, chopped
2 T. butter
3 T. all-purpose flour

1 c. milk
salt and pepper to taste
1 c. shredded Cheddar cheese
2 to 3 c. mixed vegetables,
  cooked
1/4 c. sesame seed

Combine rice, egg, Parmesan cheese and parsley; pat into the bottom
and up the sides of an ungreased 9" pie pan. Bake at 350 degrees for
10 minutes; set aside. Melt butter in a saucepan over medium heat;
whisk in flour and milk until smooth and thickened. Season to taste
with salt and pepper; stir in Cheddar cheese until melted. Remove from
heat; set aside. Fill crust with vegetables; sprinkle with sesame seed.
Pour cheese sauce on top; bake at 350 until bubbly and firm, about
15 minutes. Set aside for 10 minutes; cut into wedges to serve. Makes
6 to 8 servings.

Add some shelves inside a
fireplace mantel for a
one-of-a-kind bookcase
or shadowbox to display
favorite pottery.

Fast & Easy Zucchini Pie

Doreen DeRosa
New Castle, PA

Ready in no time!

4 c. zucchini, thinly sliced
1 c. onion, chopped
1/4 to 1/2 c. butter
2 eggs, beaten
2 T. dried parsley
1/4 t. dried oregano
1/4 t. dried basil

1/4 t. pepper
1/4 t. garlic powder
1 t. salt
1 c. mozzarella cheese, grated
8-oz. tube refrigerated crescent
   rolls, separated
2 t. mustard

Sauté zucchini and onion in butter for 10 minutes; remove from heat and set aside. Whisk the next 8 ingredients together; stir in mozzarella cheese. Fold in zucchini mixture; set aside. Line the bottom and sides of an ungreased 10" pie pan with crescent rolls; pinch seams to seal. Brush with mustard; pour egg and zucchini mixture into crust. Bake at 350 degrees until set, about 17 to 20 minutes; cover crust with aluminum foil during last 10 minutes of baking time. Makes 8 servings.

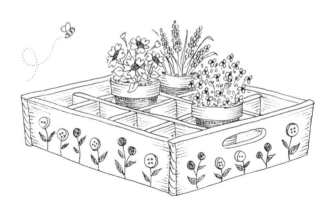

Wooden crates make terrific organizers. All those nooks & crannies are great for holding silverware or desk supplies.

Yam Risotto

Stephanie Moon
Nampa, ID

*This creamy dish has an unexpected yet delicious flavor
thanks to the yams. You can also make it a one-dish meal
by just adding cooked shredded chicken or pork.*

2 T. butter
1 shallot, minced
1 clove garlic, minced
3/4 c. Arborio rice, uncooked
1 c. canned yams, mashed
3 c. chicken broth, divided

1/4 t. cinnamon
1/4 t. salt
1/8 t. pepper
3 T. toasted pine nuts or
   pumpkin seeds

Melt butter in a saucepan; add shallot and garlic. Sauté for one minute
or until soft; stir in rice. Heat for one minute; mix in yams and 1/2 cup
chicken broth. Heat until liquid is absorbed; stir in additional 1/2 cup
broth. Continue heating for 15 minutes, stirring constantly; add broth,
1/2 cup at a time, as previous additions have been absorbed. Remove
from heat; stir in cinnamon, salt, pepper and pine nuts or pumpkin
seeds. Serve warm. Serves 4.

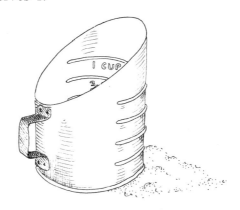

Keep a couple of stacked wooden stools on the
porch for a footrest or turn them into handy
countertop caddies to keep jars of herbs
and spices close at hand.

Cheesy Spaghetti Bake

Sandy Lynch
Iroquois, SD

A no-fuss recipe...even the kids can make it.

15-oz. can creamed corn
15-oz. can corn
1-1/2 c. pasteurized processed
   cheese spread, cubed

1/2 c. onion, minced
1 c. spaghetti, uncooked and
   coarsely broken

Combine corn, cheese and onion; stir in spaghetti pieces. Pour into an ungreased 2-quart casserole dish; cover. Bake at 350 degrees for 40 minutes; remove cover. Bake for an additional 20 minutes. Serves 4.

With no effort, a painted child's chair easily becomes a charming end table!

Old-Settler Beans

Fae Harrison
Rockford, IL

Rich molasses and brown sugar combine to make this slow-cooker bean recipe one you can count on.

1/2 lb. ground beef
1/2 lb. bacon, chopped
1 onion, chopped
1/2 lb. ham, cubed
1/2 c. brown sugar, packed
1/3 c. sugar
1/4 c. barbecue sauce

1/4 c. catsup
1/3 c. molasses
16-oz. can pinto beans
15-1/2 oz. can navy beans
15-1/2 oz. can kidney beans
28-oz. can pork & beans

Brown ground beef with bacon and onion; place into a slow cooker. Add remaining ingredients; stir to mix. Heat on low setting until warmed through, about 4 hours. Serves 8 to 10.

Bring the outdoors in...a tall shutter leaning against a wall can step in to take the place of a hanging picture or hinge several shutters together for a creative room divider.

Don't forget to eat Your Veggies

Spanish Rice

Lynda McCormick
Burkburnett, TX

I love this easy stovetop version of an old favorite...you will too!

3 T. olive oil
1 c. long-cooking rice, uncooked
2 to 3 cloves garlic, minced
16-oz. can Mexican-style
   tomatoes, chopped

1/2 c. chicken broth
1/2 c. red onion, chopped
1/4 c. green pepper, chopped
1/2 c. fresh cilantro, chopped

Heat oil in a 12" skillet; add rice, heating until golden. Add garlic; sauté
for one minute. Mix in undrained tomatoes, broth, onion and green
pepper; bring to a boil. Reduce heat; cover and simmer until
rice is done, about 15 minutes. Remove from heat; stir in cilantro.
Serves 6.

Grandma Erma's Easy Corn Fritters

Jill Munoz
Henderson, NV

Handed down and time-tested, this corn fritter recipe
makes a tasty side.

1 c. all-purpose flour
1/4 c. sugar
1 t. baking powder
14-3/4 oz. can creamed corn

2 eggs
salt and pepper to taste
oil for deep frying

Combine all ingredients; set aside. Heat 1/2 inch oil in a heavy skillet;
drop batter by teaspoonfuls into hot oil. Heat until golden on both
sides, flipping if necessary. Serves 4.

Bacon-Spinach Quiche

Melanie Spendlove
Las Vegas, NV

Great paired with any pasta dish!

3 eggs, room temperature
8-oz. pkg. cream cheese,
   softened
1/2 c. milk
pepper to taste

10-oz. pkg. frozen spinach,
   thawed
1/2 lb. bacon, crisply cooked and
   crumbled
9-inch pie crust

Mix first 6 ingredients together in order listed; pour into pie crust. Cover edges with aluminum foil; bake at 350 degrees until center is set, about 45 minutes to one hour. Makes 8 servings.

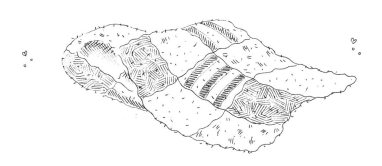

Favorite Corn Casserole

Carie Prosser
Camp Lejeune, NC

A stand-by side dish you just can't do without.

15-1/4 oz. can corn
14-3/4 oz. can creamed corn
1 c. sour cream

1 egg
7-oz. pkg. cornbread mix
1/4 c. margarine, melted

Mix all ingredients together; spread in an ungreased 13"x9" baking pan. Bake at 350 degrees for 55 minutes. Makes 12 to 15 servings.

Broccoli-Rice Delight

Kathy Achen
Las Cruces, NM

Try using half broccoli and half cauliflower for another tasty version.

2/3 c. onion, diced
2/3 c. celery, diced
2 T. oil
10-oz. pkg. frozen chopped
   broccoli, thawed
10-3/4 oz. can cream of
   mushroom soup

2/3 c. milk
1 c. water
1 c. instant rice, uncooked
8-oz. jar pasteurized processed
   cheese sauce
1 c. green chiles, chopped

Sauté onion and celery in oil until tender; add broccoli. Reduce heat; simmer for 15 minutes. Stir in remaining ingredients; bring to a boil. Remove from heat; pour into a greased 1-1/2 quart casserole dish. Bake at 350 degrees for 25 minutes. Serves 6.

Instead of a shelf to hold bathroom towels, bring in an apple-green painted basket to do the task!

Nana's Biscuits

Pamela Howe
Kingfield, ME

No one makes flaky, buttery biscuits like Nana.

4 c. all-purpose flour
6 t. baking powder
2 t. salt

1/2 c. shortening
2 c. milk
2 T. butter, melted

Combine flour, baking powder and salt; cut in shortening with 2 forks or a pastry cutter. Stir in milk; roll out to 1/2-inch thickness on a lightly floured surface. Cut with a biscuit cutter; arrange in an ungreased 13"x9" baking pan. Spread with butter; bake at 450 degrees for 15 to 20 minutes. Makes 2-1/2 dozen.

Pretty and practical, red and white linens bring extra vintage style to a country kitchen. And there's so many fun choices like turkey red, fringed or monogrammed...check out flea markets and estate sales for the best variety.

Sweet Potato Biscuits

Flo Burtnett
Gage, OK

Use a fun cookie cutter for extra-special biscuit shapes.

1-1/2 c. all-purpose flour
1 T. baking powder
1/4 t. cinnamon
1/4 t. salt
1/8 t. nutmeg

1/3 c. margarine
1 c. sweet potatoes, peeled,
   boiled and mashed
1/3 c. plus 1 T. milk, divided
Garnish: sugar

Mix flour, baking powder, cinnamon, salt and nutmeg in a medium mixing bowl; cut in margarine until coarse crumbs form. Set aside. Blend potatoes and 1/3 cup milk together; add to flour mixture. Stir with a fork until just moistened; roll dough out on a lightly floured surface to a 3/4-inch thickness; cut out with a biscuit cutter. Arrange on a greased baking sheet; brush with remaining milk. Sprinkle with sugar; bake at 425 degrees until golden, about 15 to 20 minutes. Makes one dozen.

Need a headboard? Old-fashioned picket fencing is a quick & easy solution!

Sandwich Buns

Carole Thomas
Mount Pleasant, PA

It's easy to make and serve your own homemade sandwich buns...just split open and layer with your favorite sandwich fillings.

3 pkgs. active dry yeast	1 c. shortening
4 c. warm water	2 t. salt
10 to 12 c. all-purpose flour	3/4 c. sugar
1 egg	3 T. butter, melted

Sprinkle yeast over warm water in a medium mixing bowl; set aside until foamy. Combine with remaining ingredients except butter in a very large mixing bowl; knead until smooth. Cover and let rise until double in bulk, about 45 minutes. Place one-inch round dough balls about 3 inches apart on an ungreased baking sheet; cover and let rise again, until double in bulk. Bake at 350 degrees for 20 minutes. Brush tops with butter while still warm. Makes about 3 dozen.

The tiny holes in the lids of vintage salt & pepper shakers make them the sweetest vases for small stemmed flowers.

Wholesome Bread

Janet Pastrick
Centreville, VA

A hearty loaf topped with a sprinkling of tasty tidbits.

1 pkg. active dry yeast
1/2 c. warm water
2 T. sunflower oil
1 egg
1/2 c. cottage cheese
1/4 c. honey
1 t. salt
2 to 2-1/2 c. bread flour, divided
1/2 c. whole-wheat flour

1/4 c. wheat germ
1/4 c. rye flour
1/4 c. oats, uncooked
1/4 c. cornmeal
1 egg white
2 to 4 T. sunflower kernels
1 T. sesame seed
1 t. poppy seed

Sprinkle yeast over warm water in a small mixing bowl; stir to dissolve. Set aside. Combine oil, egg, cottage cheese, honey and salt together in a large mixing bowl; stir in yeast mixture and 2 cups bread flour. Gradually stir in whole-wheat flour, wheat germ, rye flour and oats; add additional bread flour until a soft dough is achieved. Knead dough until smooth and elastic, about 10 minutes; place in a greased bowl, turning once to coat both sides. Let rise until double in bulk, about 30 minutes. Punch dough down; shape into a round loaf. Place in a 10" pie pan that has been sprinkled with cornmeal; cover loosely with greased plastic wrap. Let rise until double in bulk, about one hour. Brush top with egg white; sprinkle with sunflower kernels, sesame seed and poppy seed. Bake at 350 degrees for 35 to 40 minutes; cool on a wire rack. Serves 6.

An old tea tray can take on new life as a photo frame. Just find a tray topped with glass, gently lift one side of it and slip favorite snapshots underneath.

Hearty Harvest Loaves

Wendy Lee Paffenroth
Pine Island, NY

Topped with cream cheese, this bread is addictive!

2 eggs, beaten
2 c. sugar
1/2 c. oil
1 c. canned pumpkin
1 t. vanilla extract
2-1/4 c. all-purpose flour

1 T. pumpkin pie spice
1 t. baking soda
1/2 t. salt
1 c. chopped nuts
1 c. cranberries, chopped

Combine eggs, sugar, oil and pumpkin in a large mixing bowl; mix well. Stir in vanilla; set aside. Mix flour, pie spice, baking soda, salt and nuts in a mixing bowl; pour into pumpkin mixture, stirring well. Fold in cranberries; spoon batter evenly into 2 greased and floured 8"x4" loaf pans. Bake at 350 degrees for one hour; cool in pan for 30 to 45 minutes. Remove to a platter to slice and serve. Makes 16 servings.

A wooden window frame can become a great place to display favorite photos. Add a weave of rope or ribbon around the frame to create a criss-cross pattern to tuck photos into.

Parmesan Bread Sticks

Mary Murray
Mt. Vernon, OH

A must-have with spaghetti or lasagna and a fresh salad.

1/3 c. butter, melted
1 t. dried rosemary, crushed
1 clove garlic, minced
2-1/4 c. all-purpose flour

2 T. grated Parmesan cheese
1 T. sugar
3-1/2 t. baking powder
1 c. milk

Pour butter in a 13"x9" baking pan tilting to coat; sprinkle with rosemary and garlic. Set aside. Combine flour, cheese, sugar and baking powder; stir in milk. Turn dough onto a floured surface; knead until smooth. Roll into a 12"x6" rectangle; cut into one-inch strips. Twist each strip 6 times; place in butter mixture. Bake at 400 degrees for 20 to 25 minutes. Makes one dozen.

For a touch of nostalgia, line the inside back surfaces of cupboards or bookcases with colorful pages from old children's books.

Banana-Nut Bread

Dolly Yarborough
Broadway, NC

Small loaves make great neighbor gifts.

1-1/4 c. sugar
1/4 c. oil
1/2 c. butter
2 eggs
1-1/2 c. bananas, mashed

2 c. all-purpose flour
1/2 t. salt
1 t. baking soda
1/2 c. chopped pecans
1 t. vanilla extract

Blend sugar, oil and butter together; mix in eggs and bananas. Set aside. Combine flour, salt and baking soda; add to banana mixture. Stir in pecans and vanilla; pour into a greased and floured 9"x5" loaf pan. Bake at 300 degrees until a knife inserted in center removes clean, about one hour. Makes 8 servings.

Chocolate-Zucchini Bread

Janet Shelly
Bourbonnais, IL

For variety, substitute one tablespoon orange extract for vanilla.

3 eggs
1 c. oil
2 c. sugar
2 T. vanilla extract
2-1/2 c. all-purpose flour
1 t. salt

1-1/2 t. baking soda
2-1/2 t. baking powder
1/2 c. baking cocoa
2 c. zucchini, shredded
1 c. chopped nuts

Blend eggs, oil and sugar together in a large mixing bowl; add vanilla, flour, salt, baking soda, baking powder and cocoa, mixing well. Fold in zucchini and nuts; spoon into 2 greased 9"x5" loaf pans. Bake at 350 degrees for one hour. Makes 16 servings.

Apple Bread Pudding

Beverly Perritt
Unityville, PA

A nice switch in place of applesauce.

4 to 5 slices bread, crusts
   trimmed
1-1/2 c. applesauce
1 t. cinnamon, divided
1/8 t. nutmeg
2 t. butter

2 c. milk
2 eggs, beaten
1/2 c. sugar
1/2 t. vanilla extract
1/8 t. salt

Cube bread; layer half in a buttered 8"x8" baking pan. Set aside. Combine applesauce, 1/2 teaspoon cinnamon and nutmeg; spread over bread cubes. Layer remaining bread cubes on top; dot with butter. Whisk milk, eggs, sugar, vanilla and salt together; pour over bread mixture. Sprinkle with remaining cinnamon; cover and set aside for one to 2 hours. Bake at 350 degrees until a knife inserted in the center removes clean, about 55 to 60 minutes; cool at least 15 minutes before serving. Makes 16 servings.

Some of the best souvenirs are found at the seashore. If you want seashells to take on a white, weathered look, mix one quart of water with one cup of bleach and soak the shells 30 minutes; let dry in the sun.

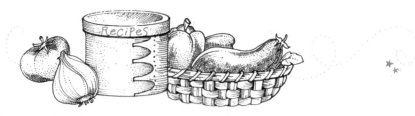

Twice-Baked Potato Casserole

Stephanie Brennan
Leawood, KS

*Sprinkle individual servings with crispy, crumbled bacon
for even more flavor.*

4 potatoes, baked and mashed
1/2 c. cream cheese
1/2 c. sour cream
1/2 c. shredded Cheddar cheese

1/4 c. onion, chopped
1/2 c. milk
salt and pepper to taste

Spread potatoes in an ungreased 13"x9" baking pan; add remaining ingredients. Stir and mix well; cover with aluminum foil. Bake at 350 degrees for 40 minutes. Serves 4.

Architectural fixtures like shower and glass door handles make super peg board knobs for holding bath towels and robes!

Scalloped Corn

Pam Berry
Huntington, IN

A true handed-down recipe from my grandmother to my mother, and shared with my daughter and me.

16-oz. can creamed corn
1/2 c. milk
1 egg, beaten
4 T. butter, melted

2 c. round buttery crackers, crushed
sugar, salt and pepper to taste

Combine all ingredients; mix well. Pour into a greased 1-1/2 quart casserole dish; bake at 350 degrees until golden, about 45 minutes. Makes 6 to 8 servings.

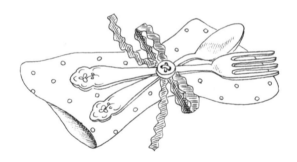

Old-Fashioned Baked Corn

Tami Bowman
Marysville, OH

I think this is the best recipe…you've got to try it.

2 16-oz. cans corn, drained
1/4 c. sugar
1/4 c. butter, melted
1/3 c. all-purpose flour

4 eggs, beaten
2/3 c. milk
8-oz. pkg. pasteurized processed cheese spread, cubed

Combine all ingredients together in a large mixing bowl; spread in an ungreased 2-quart casserole dish. Bake at 325 degrees for 45 to 55 minutes. Serves 8.

Buttery Cauliflower Casserole

Holly Sutton
Middleburgh, NY

Try American or Swiss cheese for a brand new taste.

1 head cauliflower, broken into
    flowerets
1 c. sour cream
1 c. shredded Cheddar cheese
1/2 c. round buttery crackers,
    crushed
1/4 c. green peppers, chopped
1/4 c. red peppers, chopped
1 t. salt
1/4 c. grated Parmesan cheese

Place cauliflower in a saucepan filled with one inch water; heat until tender. Drain. Stir in sour cream, cheese, crushed crackers, peppers and salt; spoon into a greased 2-quart casserole dish. Sprinkle with Parmesan cheese; bake at 325 degrees for 30 minutes. Serves 6 to 8.

Turn a pretty oval picture frame into a vanity tray in minutes! Replace the glass with a matching size mirror and it's ready to fill with make up, perfume bottles, nail polish and lotions.

Don't forget to eat your Veggies

Crispy Green Bean Bake

Tanya Duke
Bethany, OK

Try this new twist on an old favorite.

6 T. margarine, melted and
   divided
3 T. all-purpose flour
1 t. sugar
1 t. onion powder
1 c. sour cream

salt and pepper to taste
3 16-oz. cans green beans,
   drained
2 c. shredded Cheddar cheese
2 c. crispy rice cereal, crushed

Combine 3 tablespoons margarine, flour, sugar, onion powder, sour cream, salt and pepper; mix well. Stir in green beans; spread in an ungreased 13"x9" baking pan. Sprinkle with cheese; set aside. Mix cereal with remaining margarine; crumble over cheese layer. Bake at 350 degrees for 35 minutes. Serves 6.

Carrots Au Gratin

Faith Gregory
Hamilton, OH

For individual servings, spoon into au gratin dishes before baking.

2 c. carrots, thinly sliced
1/4 c. onions, minced
1/2 c. water
1/4 c. plus 3 T. butter, divided
1/4 c. all-purpose flour

1-1/2 c. milk
1/3 c. shredded Cheddar cheese
1 T. dried parsley
2 c. round buttery crackers,
   crushed

Heat carrots and onions in water until tender; drain. Add 1/4 cup butter and flour; stir in milk, heating until thickened. Remove from heat; add cheese and parsley. Pour into a greased 13"x9" baking pan; set aside. Mix remaining butter with cracker crumbs; sprinkle on top. Bake at 370 degrees for 20 minutes. Serves 4.

Creamy Scalloped Potatoes

Delinda Blakney
Dallas, GA

*Who can resist scalloped potatoes? They go with
practically any main dish!*

1/4 c. fresh parsley, minced
1 t. pepper
10-3/4 oz. can cream of chicken
   soup
1/2 c. milk

1 t. salt
4 c. potatoes, peeled, sliced and
   divided
1 onion, chopped and divided

Mix parsley, pepper, soup, milk and salt together; set aside. Layer half
the potatoes in a buttered 1-1/2 quart casserole dish; top with 1/2 cup
onion. Repeat layers; spread soup mixture on top. Cover; bake at
350 degrees until potatoes are soft, about one hour. Serves 4.

*Don't pass up blue-tinted canning jars that can be
filled with sand and flickering votives. Perfect for
giving windowboxes color and sparkle during
the winter.*

It's six o'clock...

Mom, what's for dinner?

½ T. dry mustard
½ T. paprika
2½ c. milk
T. worcestershire

flour
butter
T. salt
¼ t. pepper

Prepar
sprea
Set a

eat
serole

noodles
shroom soup
milk
ans tuna, dra
can peas, dra
ine all ing
at until warme

7 oz. pkg.   nbread mix
10¾ oz Cream of celery
1 onion, diced
2 T. butter
2 boneless breasts
10¾ oz Can Cream of
Chicken soup

ead
Serve

Country Kitchen Beef & Vegetables

Mary Jo Hanson
Centerville, WA

This recipe came about using a little creativity and some leftovers.
Now, it's a regular request at our house!

1-1/2 lbs. stew beef, cubed
1-lb. pkg. sliced mushrooms
1 c. green onions, sliced
2 T. olive oil
1/4 c. red wine or beef broth
1-1/2 c. beef broth
1 T. minced garlic

6-oz. can tomato paste
1/2 t. dried parsley
1/2 t. dried thyme
14-1/2 oz. can diced tomatoes
salt and pepper to taste
16-oz. pkg. egg noodles, cooked
2 T. butter, melted

Brown beef with mushrooms and onions in olive oil and red wine in
a Dutch oven; add remaining ingredients except noodles and butter.
Bring to a boil; reduce heat and simmer for one hour. To serve, spoon
beef mixture over warm buttered noodles. Serves 6 to 8.

Because they're so tall, sap buckets are great
hanging on the wall waiting to hold mail. Mark
one "in" and the another one "out" to keep
the mail and newspapers tidy.

Oven-Easy Beef Bake

Nancy Husted
North Chelmsford, MA

So simple to make, you'll find yourself turning to this recipe again and again.

1-1/2 lbs. stew beef, cubed
2 T. oil
10-1/2 oz. can mushroom gravy
12-oz. can tomato juice

1/2 c. water
1-1/2 oz. pkg. onion soup mix
4 potatoes, peeled and quartered

Brown beef in oil; drain and set aside. Combine gravy, tomato juice, water and onion soup mix in a stockpot; bring to a boil. Reduce heat; add beef and simmer for 5 minutes. Remove from heat; set aside. Arrange potatoes in a greased 13"x9" baking pan; pour beef mixture on top. Cover with aluminum foil; bake at 350 degrees for 2 hours. Makes 6 servings.

Game boards give a great splash of color to plain walls. Try grouping several together to show off a fun collection.

Skillet Honey Chicken

Jennifer Eveland-Kupp
Reading, PA

A tender, juicy chicken dish easily made on your stovetop.

2 T. butter
2 T. honey
4 to 6 boneless, skinless chicken
    breasts

1/2 c. orange juice

Melt butter with honey in a 12" skillet; add chicken. Brown both sides over medium heat until juices run clear when chicken is pierced with a fork; reduce heat to low. Pour orange juice on top; cover and heat for 10 minutes. Uncover and heat until juices reduce to a glaze. Serves 4 to 6.

Don't pass up a stylish old-fashioned fan...their retro good looks bring a fresh breeze to any room.

Easy Sweet & Sour Chicken

Sandra Nakagawa
Honolulu, HI

Served on a bed of rice or crunchy chow mein noodles, this is a meal the whole family will love.

8-oz. bottle Russian dressing
1-1/2 oz. pkg. onion soup mix
1/3 c. apricot jam

2-1/2 to 3 lbs. boneless, skinless chicken breasts, sliced lengthwise

Whisk the first 3 ingredients in a mixing bowl; set aside. Arrange chicken in an ungreased 13"x9" baking pan; pour dressing mixture on top. Bake at 350 degrees for one hour or until juices run clear when chicken is pierced with a fork. Makes 4 to 6 servings.

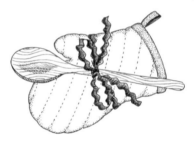

Cranberry Chicken

Denise Eldridge
Kenduskeag, ME

Try using maple-flavored bacon for a tasty change.

4 slices bacon
4 boneless, skinless chicken
   breasts
10-oz. jar cocktail onions,
   drained

1-1/2 oz. pkg. onion soup mix
16-oz. can whole berry
   cranberry sauce
1/3 c. water
1/4 t. dried thyme

Cook bacon until crisply cooked; crumble and set aside. Reserve drippings in skillet. Brown chicken in same skillet; remove from heat. Combine remaining ingredients; mix well. Pour over chicken; simmer, covered, for 40 minutes or until juices run clear when chicken is pierced with a fork. Serves 4.

Tuna Noodle Casserole

Jan Shields
Parma, OH

A true family favorite recipe you just can't beat!

16-oz. pkg. wide egg noodles,
    cooked
2 10-3/4 oz. cans cream of
    mushroom soup

1-1/3 c. milk
2 6-oz. cans tuna, drained
15-oz. can peas, drained

Combine all ingredients in large stockpot; heat until warmed through,
stirring often. Serves 8.

When looking for added color in any room,
toss in some pillows decked out in vintage fabrics,
fringe and buttons.

Hot Chicken Salad

Lynne Davisson
Cable, OH

A tried & true favorite recipe that's been shared with 3 generations.

1/4 c. margarine
1/2 c. onion, chopped
4-oz. jar red pimentos
6-oz. pkg. slivered almonds
1/3 green pepper, diced
4-oz. can mushroom pieces,
   drained

1 c. celery, chopped
4 c. cooked chicken, diced
1 c. mayonnaise
10-3/4 oz. can cream of celery
   soup
1 t. salt
1 c. corn flake cereal, crushed

Melt margarine in a large skillet; add the next 6 ingredients. Sauté until vegetables are tender; place into an ungreased 13"x9" baking pan. Add chicken, mayonnaise, soup and salt; mix well. Sprinkle with crushed corn flake cereal; bake at 350 degrees for 30 minutes. Makes 10 servings.

Old linens can be found at most tag sales, but can often be slightly worn. No worries...because they're already less-than-perfect, they're perfect spread over an outside porch table.

Cabbage Roll Casserole

Dianne Gregory
Sheridan, AR

A tasty favorite, without the fuss!

2 lbs. ground beef, browned
1 c. onion, chopped
29-oz. can tomato sauce
3-1/2 lbs. cabbage, chopped

1 c. instant rice, uncooked
1 t. salt
14-oz. can beef broth

Combine first 6 ingredients in a large mixing bowl; spread in an ungreased 13"x9" baking pan. Pour broth on top; cover with aluminum foil. Bake at 350 degrees for one hour; uncover and stir. Recover and bake 30 additional minutes. Makes 12 servings.

A vintage handkerchief makes a sweet nursery valance when draped over a tension or café rod.

Roasted Eggplant Parmesan

Deborah Byrne
Clinton, CT

I still can't believe I got my family to eat eggplant! This is such a fabulous recipe...how could they not love it?

2-1/2 lbs. eggplant, cut into
   1/2-inch slices
1/4 c. olive oil
1/2 t. salt, divided
28-oz. can crushed tomatoes
1/4 t. pepper

1/2 t. Italian seasoning
1/8 t. red pepper flakes
2 c. shredded mozzarella cheese,
   divided
1/2 c. grated Parmesan cheese

Arrange a single layer eggplant on 2 ungreased baking sheets; brush with olive oil. Sprinkle with 1/4 teaspoon salt; bake at 450 degrees for 15 minutes. Flip slices; bake for an additional 10 minutes. Set aside. Combine tomatoes, pepper, remaining salt, Italian seasoning and red pepper flakes in a skillet; heat until thickened, about 20 minutes. Layer half the eggplant in an ungreased 2-1/2 quart casserole dish; top with half the tomato mixture. Sprinkle with one cup mozzarella cheese; repeat layers. Top with Parmesan cheese; bake at 400 degrees until bubbly, about 10 minutes. Let stand for at least 10 minutes before serving. Serves 4 to 6.

Second hand objects make
first-rate treasures.

—Unknown

Mom's Macaroni & Cheese

April Farley
Lowell, MA

A warm, tasty dinner that'll please the kids as well as mom & dad.

1-1/2 c. elbow macaroni,
   uncooked
4 T. all-purpose flour
4 T. butter
1-1/2 t. salt
1/4 t. pepper

1/2 T. dry mustard
1/2 T. paprika
2-1/2 c. milk
1 T. Worcestershire sauce
10-oz. pkg. sharp Cheddar
   cheese, cubed

Prepare macaroni according to package directions; spread in an ungreased 13"x9" baking pan. Set aside. Combine remaining ingredients in a heavy saucepan; heat until melted and smooth, stirring often. Pour over macaroni; bake at 400 degrees for 30 minutes. Serves 4.

Put a candlestick to use as a clever lamp base. Lamp kits are available at most hardware stores and take hardly any time at all to put together.

Golden Baked French Toast, page 12

Swirled Coffee Cake, page 21

Early Morning Breakfast, page 29

Always-Requested Spinach Dip, page 48

Friendship Cheese Ball, page 34

Crunchy Bacon-Cheese Dip, page 35

Cream of Tomato Soup, page 61

Fresh Cranberry Salad, page 83

Chicken & Dumplings, page 73

Cabbage Roll Casserole, page 124

Bacon-Spinach Quiche, page 102

Marvelous Meatloaf, page 127

Freeze & Bake Lasagna, page 146

Easy Sweet & Sour Chicken, page 121

Blue Goose Pie, page 157

Banana-Chocolate Chip
Cookies, page 172

Strawberry Bread, page 7

Aunt Ceil's Refrigerated Pickles, page 192

Homemade Strawberry Jam, page 185

It's six o'clock... Mom, what's for dinner?

Marvelous Meatloaf

Amy Herman
Sandwich, MA

Thick slices served with mashed potatoes...that's comfort food!

3/4 c. bread crumbs
3/4 c. milk
1-1/2 lbs. ground beef
1 onion, chopped
1 t. salt

1 t. pepper
1 T. Worcestershire sauce
1/2 c. catsup
2 T. mustard
2 T. brown sugar, packed

Combine bread crumbs and milk in a large mixing bowl; add the next 5 ingredients, mixing well. Place into an ungreased 9"x5" loaf pan; set aside. Stir catsup, mustard and sugar together; spoon over meatloaf. Bake at 375 degrees for one hour. Makes 8 servings.

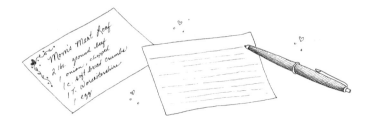

Applesauce Meatloaf

Amy Sund
Winner, SD

This makes terrific sandwiches the next day.

1 lb. ground beef
3/4 c. applesauce
1/2 c. bread crumbs
1 t. salt
1/4 t. seasoned salt

2 eggs, beaten
1/2 c. onion, chopped
1/4 c. catsup
1/4 c. brown sugar, packed
1/8 c. mustard

Mix the first 7 ingredients together; spoon into an ungreased 9"x5" loaf pan. Set aside. Combine catsup, sugar and mustard; spread over meatloaf. Bake at 350 degrees for one hour. Makes 8 servings.

Skillet Supper

Sharon Crider
Lebanon, MO

Add a side of fresh fruit for a quick & easy dinner.

1-1/2 T. butter
3 potatoes, peeled, thinly sliced
   and divided
1/2 c. green onions, chopped
   and divided
1/2 c. green pepper, chopped
   and divided

2 c. cooked ham, diced
1/2 t. salt
pepper to taste
3 eggs, slightly beaten
1/2 c. shredded Cheddar cheese

Melt butter in a 10" skillet; layer with half of the next 4 ingredients. Sprinkle with salt and pepper; repeat layers. Cover and heat until potatoes are tender, about 20 to 25 minutes; pour eggs on top. Cover and heat until set, about 17 minutes; uncover and sprinkle with cheese. Recover and heat until melted; cut into wedges to serve. Serves 4.

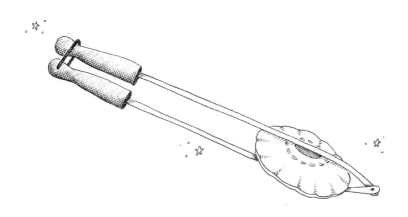

Use an old iron gate for a fireplace screen or hinge together sections of wooden shutters...so eye-catching!

Broccoli-Ham Ring

Cathy Burgess
Elkins, WV

This dinner always looks like you've baked all day, but it's really very easy to make. I just prepare it in the morning, and then pop it in the oven before friends arrive.

1/4 lb. cooked ham, chopped
1/4 lb. broccoli, chopped
1 onion, chopped
2/3 c. shredded Swiss cheese
2 T. Dijon mustard
1/2 c. fresh parsley, chopped
1 t. lemon juice
2 8-oz. tubes refrigerated
   crescent rolls, separated

Mix ham, broccoli, onion, cheese, mustard, parsley and lemon juice together; set aside. Spread out crescent rolls with bases overlapping about 1/4 inch on each side in the center and points toward the outside on an ungreased pizza pan; spoon ham mixture into the center of each base. Fold points of crescent rolls back over filling; tuck under bases in the center, pinching to seal. Bake at 350 degrees for 20 to 25 minutes. Serves 8.

Turn leaded or stained-glass windows into coffee tables in a flash...just add legs!

Easy Overnight Lasagna

Krista Starnes
Beaufort, SC

My best friend gave me this recipe and it's so easy, we make it all the time. It seems I'm always asked to share the recipe, which I gladly do.

1 lb. ground Italian sausage,
   browned
26-oz. jar spaghetti sauce
1 c. water
15-oz. container ricotta cheese
2 T. fresh chives, chopped
1/2 t. dried oregano

1 egg
8-oz. pkg. lasagna noodles,
   uncooked and divided
4 c. shredded mozzarella cheese,
   divided
2 T. grated Parmesan cheese

Combine sausage, spaghetti sauce and water in a 12" skillet; simmer for 5 minutes. In a medium mixing bowl, add ricotta cheese, chives, oregano and egg; mix well. Set aside. Spread 1-1/2 cups meat sauce in the bottom of an ungreased 13"x9" baking pan; top with half the noodles. Spread with half the ricotta mixture; sprinkle with half the mozzarella cheese. Repeat layers. Pour remaining meat sauce over the top; sprinkle with Parmesan cheese. Cover with aluminum foil; refrigerate overnight. Uncover dish; bake at 350 degrees for 50 minutes to one hour or until noodles are tender. Cover; let stand 15 minutes before serving. Serves 6.

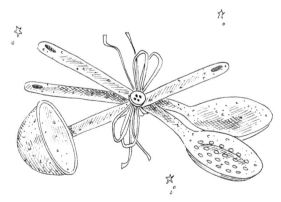

A newel post from an antique staircase makes a beautiful and sturdy plant stand.

Italian Supper Casserole

Wendy Lee Paffenroth
Pine Island, NY

When my kids were small and it seemed we were always on the go,
I made a lot of casseroles like this one. Sometimes on a Sunday
afternoon I'd put together 3 or 4 different casseroles and freeze them
for busy nights. That way, we always ate dinner together as a family.

1-1/2 lbs. ground beef
1 onion, chopped
1 green pepper, sliced
28-oz. can crushed tomatoes
1-1/2 c. water
1 T. dried oregano

salt and pepper to taste
8-oz. pkg. wide egg noodles,
   cooked, rinsed and divided
1 c. shredded Cheddar cheese
4-oz. can sliced mushrooms,
   drained

Brown ground beef with onion; drain. Add green pepper; heat
until tender. Pour in tomatoes and water; add oregano, salt and
pepper, stirring often. Remove from heat; set aside. Spread half the
noodles in an ungreased 13"x9" baking pan; layer half the ground
beef mixture on top. Sprinkle with half the cheese; repeat layers.
Spread mushrooms on top; bake at 350 degrees for 20 to 30 minutes.
Serves 6.

Give a tired screen door a facelift with a little
paint and a new screen. For a clever twist, hang it
between rooms as a puppy gate.

Sausage-Stuffing Balls

Susan Young
Madison, AL

This recipe has been in my recipe box for nearly 35 years...it always reminds me of wonderful meals with family & friends.

1 lb. ground sausage, browned
1/2 c. celery, chopped
1/2 c. onion, diced
8-oz. pkg. stuffing mix
1/2 c. cranberries, chopped
1 egg, beaten
1 c. chicken broth
1/2 c. butter, melted

Place sausage, celery and onion in a skillet; heat until vegetables are tender. Transfer to a bowl; toss with stuffing mix. Stir in cranberries, egg, chicken broth and butter; mix well. Shape into 8 to 10 balls; arrange on an ungreased baking sheet. Bake at 325 degrees for 30 minutes. Makes 8 to 10 servings.

Don't forget the porch...add a vintage picture or two, old signs and architectural salvage pieces to give it an old-fashioned feel.

It's six o'clock... Mom, what's for dinner?

The Best Pork Chops

Malinda Gillespie
Birmingham, AL

My husband loves these...they're so tender they fall off the bone!

2 onions, thinly sliced
1/4 c. butter
6 pork chops
salt and pepper to taste
1 c. chicken broth

1 c. white wine or chicken broth
1 bay leaf
4 carrots, peeled and sliced
3 potatoes, peeled and quartered

Sauté onions in butter in a 12" skillet until golden; add pork chops. Sprinkle with salt and pepper; heat until browned on both sides. Pour in broth and wine; add bay leaf. Cover and simmer for 1-1/2 hours; add vegetables. Cover and simmer for an additional 1-1/2 hours. Serves 6.

Combine a discarded window frame with a windowbox to create a whimsical spot on a garden shed. Don't forget to fill the box with lots of blooms!

Chicken & Broccoli Alfredo

Kari Delgado
Chandler, AZ

If your family doesn't like broccoli, try adding slices of
sauteed sweet red pepper or cherry tomatoes.

8-oz. pkg. linguine, uncooked
1 c. broccoli flowerets
2 T. butter
1-lb. pkg. boneless, skinless
   chicken breasts, cubed

10-3/4 oz. can cream of
   mushroom soup
1/2 c. milk
1/2 c. grated Parmesan cheese
1/4 t. pepper

Cook linguine according to package directions; add broccoli during the last 4 minutes of cooking time. Drain; set aside. Heat butter in a 12" skillet; add chicken. Heat until juices run clear when chicken is pierced with a fork; reduce heat. Stir in soup, milk, cheese, pepper and linguine mixture; heat through. Serves 4.

Stone urns are not only great filled with flowers,
they make pretty bird baths too!

It's six o'clock... Mom, what's for dinner?

Slow-Cooker Lasagna

Debra Donaldson
Florala, AL

So much easier, but just as wonderful as baked lasagna.

1 lb. ground beef
1/2 c. onion, chopped
1 t. minced garlic
16-oz. can tomato sauce
1 c. water
6-oz. can tomato paste
4-oz. can sliced mushrooms,
    drained

1 t. salt
1 t. dried oregano
8-oz. pkg. lasagna noodles,
    uncooked and divided
2 c. shredded mozzarella cheese
12-oz. container cottage cheese
1/2 c. grated Parmesan cheese

Brown beef with onion and garlic; remove from heat. Place in a large mixing bowl; add tomato sauce, water, tomato paste, mushrooms, salt and oregano, mixing well. Spread 1/4 of the meat sauce in the bottom of a 5-quart slow cooker; arrange 1/3 of the noodles over the sauce, breaking if necessary. Combine the cheeses together; spoon 1/3 over the noodle layer. Repeat layers twice; top with remaining meat sauce. Cover and heat on low until noodles are tender, about 4 to 5 hours. Serves 8.

A wobbly chair can still be a flea market treasure...steady the bottom of the troublesome leg with a slice of cork from an old bottle stopper.

Asparagus Pasta

Brandi Talton
Blackshear, GA

For a new taste, substitute shrimp or scallops for chicken.

5 to 6 boneless, skinless chicken
    breasts, sliced
1 T. olive oil
15-oz. can asparagus spears
1/3 c. sherry or chicken broth
10-3/4 oz. can cream of chicken
    or cream of mushroom soup

2 t. garlic powder
1/2 c. shredded sharp Cheddar
    cheese
16-oz. pkg. angel hair pasta,
    cooked

Sauté chicken in olive oil until juices run clear when pierced with a fork; add asparagus liquid, sherry or chicken broth, soup and garlic powder. Reduce heat and simmer until creamy, about 20 minutes. Add cheese and asparagus spears; heat for 10 additional minutes. Serve over warm pasta. Serves 6.

Use crystal or brass doorknobs as curtain tiebacks. Smaller knobs can be screwed directly into the wall to become lovely dish-towel hangers in the kitchen.

Hearty Pork Chop Dinner

Heather Maline
Phillips, NE

Minimal effort and the kids love it!

4 pork chops
2 T. olive oil
1 sweet onion, sliced into rings
salt and pepper to taste

26-oz. jar spaghetti sauce
1/4 c. brown sugar, packed
16-oz. pkg. spiral pasta, cooked

Brown pork chops in olive oil in a 12" skillet over medium heat; drain. Reduce heat to medium-low; spread onion rings on top. Season with salt and pepper. Whisk spaghetti sauce and brown sugar together; pour over pork chops. Cover and simmer for 45 minutes; serve over warm pasta. Serves 4.

Need a fast and easy curtain? Stitch ribbon tabs onto linen placemats!

Chicken & Cornbread Bake

Tracy Bruce
McChord AFB, WA

Tender chicken between layers of buttery cornbread.

2 to 3 7-oz. pkgs. cornbread
   mix
1 onion, diced
2 T. butter
2 boneless, skinless chicken
   breasts, cooked and cubed
10-3/4 oz. can cream of chicken
   soup
10-3/4 oz. can cream of celery
   soup
10-1/2 oz. can chicken broth
3 hard-boiled eggs, peeled and
   sliced

Prepare cornbread according to package directions; crumble and set aside. Sauté onion in butter until tender; add cornbread, mixing well. Remove from heat; spread half the cornbread mixture in an ungreased 13"x9" baking pan. Set aside. Combine chicken, soups and broth; pour over cornbread mixture. Arrange egg slices on top; spread remaining cornbread mixture over the top. Bake at 325 degrees until heated through, about 20 to 30 minutes. Serves 8 to 10.

Create a unique vintage-style night light...tuck a small battery-operated candlestick light inside an old-fashioned tin grater.

It's six o'clock... Mom, what's for dinner?

Flaky Chicken Pot Pie

Terri Childress
Staunton, VA

A golden crust over chicken and vegetables...oh-so good.

2 15-oz. cans mixed
   vegetables, drained
10-oz. can chicken
1/2 t. garlic powder

1/2 c. milk
2 10-3/4 oz. cans cream of
   chicken soup

Combine ingredients in a large mixing bowl; spread into a greased 13"x9" baking pan. Spread topping evenly on top; bake at 400 degrees until golden, about 30 to 35 minutes. Serves 6.

Topping:

1/2 c. butter
1 c. all-purpose flour
1 c. milk

1/4 t. pepper
1/2 t. salt
2 t. baking powder

Melt butter in a 2-quart saucepan; remove from heat. Whisk in flour until smooth; add remaining ingredients, mixing well. Mixture may be lumpy.

An oh-so easy slipcover! Just slide a pretty handstitched pillowcase over the back of a wooden chair.

Spicy Beef Casserole

Karen Williams
Port Orchard, WA

Ideal for toting to an office potluck or luncheon.

1 lb. ground beef	1/4 c. all-purpose flour
1 onion, chopped	1/2 t. salt
salt and pepper to taste	4 eggs
4-oz. can diced green chiles	1-1/2 c. milk
3 c. shredded Cheddar cheese, divided	1/2 t. hot pepper sauce

Brown beef with onion; drain. Sprinkle with salt and pepper; set aside. Layer chiles in an ungreased 13"x9" baking pan; top with half the beef mixture and half the cheese. Repeat layers; set aside. Combine remaining ingredients; pour on top. Bake at 350 degrees until set, about 45 minutes. Serves 6.

Cut and glue pictures to the centers of mismatched saucers for the sweetest picture frames. Line up several on a cupboard shelf or mantel.

Pastisio

Lindsey Hignite
Morrisville, NC

Think of this as a Greek lasagna...filled with wonderful ingredients and absolutely delicious!

1 lb. ground beef, browned
1 onion, chopped
1 clove garlic, minced
8-oz. can tomato sauce
1 t. dried oregano
1 t. salt
1/2 t. cinnamon
2 c. elbow macaroni, uncooked
  and divided

1/4 c. butter
3 T. all-purpose flour
1/4 t. pepper
1/4 t. nutmeg
2 c. milk
2 eggs
1/4 c. grated Parmesan cheese

Combine beef, onion and garlic in a skillet; heat until onion and garlic are tender. Stir in tomato sauce, oregano, salt and cinnamon; simmer for 5 minutes. Set aside. Spread one cup macaroni in a greased 8"x8" baking pan; cover with meat sauce. Top with remaining macaroni; set aside. Melt butter in a saucepan; whisk in flour, pepper and nutmeg until smooth. Gradually pour in milk; heat until thickened. Remove from heat; whisk in eggs and Parmesan cheese. Pour over macaroni; bake at 350 degrees for 45 minutes or until top is golden. Serves 4.

HOMEMADE

Decoupage color copies of colorful barkcloth to an old pail and fill with flowers, napkins or utensils...a great way to add color to any table.

Turkey Club Bake

Jackie Smulski
Lyons, IL

A favorite sandwich becomes a hearty dinner!

2 c. biscuit baking mix
1/2 c. mayonnaise, divided
1/3 c. milk
2 c. cooked turkey, cubed
2 green onions, sliced

6 slices bacon, crisply cooked
  and crumbled
1 tomato, chopped
2/3 c. shredded Colby Jack
  cheese

Combine biscuit mix, 1/3 cup mayonnaise and milk until a soft dough forms; press into a 12"x8" rectangle. Arrange on a lightly buttered baking sheet; bake at 450 degrees until golden, about 8 to 10 minutes. Mix turkey, onions, bacon and remaining mayonnaise; spread over crust. Sprinkle with tomato and cheese; bake until cheese melts, about 5 to 6 minutes. Serves 6.

How smart! Turn an old woven clothes hamper into a handy umbrella stand.

Chicken & Ham Roll-Ups

Amanda Walton
Marysville, OH

For variety, spoon small amounts of chopped broccoli, spinach or onions over the chicken before rolling up and then bake as directed.

4 boneless, skinless chicken
  breasts, split open
4 slices deli ham
1-1/2 c. shredded Colby Jack
  cheese

10-3/4 oz. can cream of chicken
  soup
1 c. milk
8-oz. pkg. medium egg noodles,
  cooked

Arrange open chicken breasts in a 13"x9" baking pan sprayed with non-stick vegetable spray; layer each with one slice ham. Sprinkle with cheese. Roll up each breast, lengthwise; secure closed with toothpicks. Set aside. Combine soup and milk; pour over roll-ups. Cover with aluminum foil; bake at 425 degrees for 45 minutes. Divide cooked noodles equally among 4 serving plates. Arrange one roll-up on each bed of noodles; spoon remaining soup mixture on top. Remove toothpicks before serving. Serves 4.

Search flea market tables filled with dishes for unique candleholders. A tall hobnail cup filled with buttons securely holds a taper candle, while a smaller teacup is ideal for a votive.

Freeze & Bake Lasagna

Lucy Sisson
Monroe, LA

*This recipe is enough to fill 2 loaf pans...one for tonight
and another for next week.*

28-oz. jar spaghetti sauce
1-lb. pkg. ground beef, browned
8-oz. jar mushroom pieces,
    drained
16-oz. container ricotta cheese
1 egg
1 T. Italian seasoning

8 lasagna noodles, uncooked
    and divided
2 c. shredded Monterey Jack
    cheese
2 c. shredded mozzarella cheese

Combine sauce, beef and mushrooms; set aside. Mix ricotta cheese,
egg and Italian seasoning together; set aside. Layer as follows in
each of 2 ungreased 9"x5" loaf pans: one cup meat sauce, 2 lasagna
noodles, 1/2 cup ricotta cheese mixture, 1/2 cup Monterey Jack cheese
and 1/2 cup mozzarella cheese. Repeat layers until all ingredients are
gone. Cover with aluminum foil; bake at 350 degrees for 1-1/2 hours.
Serve one and set other aside until cool; place in freezer until needed.
Each serves 4.

*Secure small glass knobs to a wooden rolling pin
and slip into a vintage rolling pin holder.
So nice for keeping pot holders and
measuring spoons handy.*

Layered Cheesy Pasta Bake

Jessica Parker
Mulvane, KS

A tossed salad and bread sticks are all you need
to complete this meal.

1 onion, chopped
2 cloves garlic, chopped
1 T. oil
1-1/2 lbs. ground beef, browned
14-oz. can stewed tomatoes
16-oz. jar spaghetti sauce
12-oz. can mushroom stems
   and pieces

16-oz. pkg. elbow macaroni,
   cooked and divided
2 c. sour cream, divided
4 c. shredded Colby Jack cheese,
   divided

Sauté onion and garlic in oil in a 12" skillet until tender; add beef, tomatoes, spaghetti sauce and mushrooms. Bring to a boil; reduce heat and simmer for 20 minutes. Remove from heat; set aside. Spread half the macaroni in an ungreased 13"x9" baking pan; top with half the beef mixture, half the sour cream and half the cheese. Repeat layers. Cover with aluminum foil; bake at 350 degrees for 45 minutes. Serves 8.

Heavy architectural stars make the best paper weights!

Confetti Ziti

Vanessa Longenecker
Lancaster, PA

A colorful twist to a traditional dish.

16-oz. pkg. ziti, cooked
1-1/2 c. red pepper, sliced
1-1/2 c. yellow pepper, sliced
2 c. shredded Cheddar cheese
2 c. shredded Monterey Jack
   cheese
28-oz. can whole tomatoes

1 t. salt
1 t. pepper
1 c. half-and-half
1/2 c. seasoned bread crumbs

Combine ziti, peppers, cheese, tomatoes, salt and pepper in a greased 13"x9" baking pan. Pour half-and-half over the top; cover with aluminum foil. Bake at 350 degrees for 30 minutes; remove cover. Sprinkle with bread crumbs; bake, uncovered, for an additional 30 minutes. Serves 12.

Brighten up a corner of the porch by framing old flower seed packets or feed sacks.

Inside-Out Ravioli

Susan Biffignani
Fenton, MO

Funny name, terrific dish!

1 lb. ground beef
1 onion, chopped
1 clove garlic, minced
5 T. oil, divided
10-oz. pkg. frozen chopped
    spinach, thawed, drained
    and cooked
16-oz. jar spaghetti sauce
8-oz. can tomato sauce
6-oz. can tomato paste

1/2 t. salt
1/8 t. pepper
1 c. water
 7-oz. pkg. elbow macaroni,
    cooked
1/2 c. bread crumbs
1 c. shredded sharp Cheddar
    cheese
2 eggs, beaten

Brown beef with onion and garlic in one tablespoon oil; remove from
heat and set aside. Combine spinach, spaghetti sauce, tomato sauce,
tomato paste, salt and pepper; stir into beef mixture. Return to heat
and simmer for 10 minutes; set aside. In another bowl, mix remaining
ingredients together; spread in an ungreased 13"x9" baking pan. Top
with meat sauce; bake at 350 degrees for 30 minutes. Let stand
10 minutes before serving. Serves 8 to 10.

*Grab an orchard
ladder when spotted
at a yard or tag
sale...so handy for
hanging towels
or quilts.*

Zucchini Frittata

Liliana Vernon
Rathdrum, ID

Got a bumper zucchini crop? Try this for dinner tonight.

2 zucchini, thinly sliced
1/2 onion, diced
2 T. oil
6 eggs, beaten
1/2 c. half-and-half
1/4 t. salt
1/4 t. pepper
1 tomato, chopped
1 c. cream cheese, cubed and
  divided
2 to 3 slices whole-wheat bread,
  cubed

Sauté zucchini and onion in oil; set aside. Blend eggs, half-and-half, salt and pepper together in a large mixing bowl; stir in zucchini mixture, tomato, 3/4 cup cream cheese and bread cubes. Set aside. Place remaining cream cheese in a greased 13"x9" baking pan; pour egg mixture over the top. Bake at 350 degrees until center is set, about 30 to 45 minutes; let stand 5 to 10 minutes before serving. Serves 8.

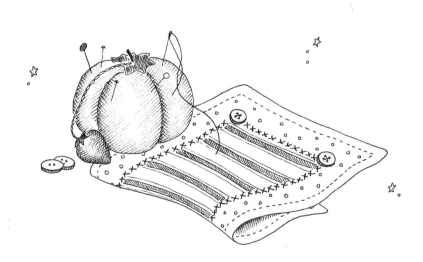

Don't pass up a wire dish drainer...what a clever way to organize file folders!

No dessert 'til you **clean your plate!**

brown butter

Gently toss apples 9" pie cru

cinnamon 1 t. cinna

pie crust

sugar a

n the s

topping

apples

kitchen of
Grandma

spiced cake Mix
cooking oats, uncooke

OPTION:
1 c. chopped n

packed

Recipe Cake Mix Brownies

½ c. margerine

50 caramels
5 oz. can evap. milk
18½ oz. pkg German
Chocolate Cake Mix
ed nuts
chips

Lemony Chocolate Chippers

Wynter Nichols
Salinas, CA

*A tasty cookie that may be made ahead of time
and frozen until needed.*

3/4 c. butter, softened
1 c. sugar
2 eggs
2 t. lemon extract
2 c. all-purpose flour

1/2 t. baking soda
1/2 t. cinnamon
2 c. mini semi-sweet chocolate
   chips

Cream butter with sugar in a large mixing bowl until light and fluffy;
blend in eggs and lemon extract. Set aside. Combine flour, baking soda
and cinnamon in a small bowl; mix into sugar mixture. Fold in
chocolate chips; mix well. Drop by teaspoonfuls onto ungreased baking
sheets; bake at 300 degrees for 12 to 15 minutes. Cool on baking
sheets for 3 minutes; remove to a wire rack to cool completely. Makes
about 2 dozen.

*If the doors are missing on a cupboard that's a
great buy, snap it up...it'll be perfect for showing
off favorite collectibles!*

no *dessert* 'til you clean your plate!

Frosted Orange Cookies

DarLinda Adams
Orlando, FL

A delightfully soft old-fashioned cookie.

2 navel oranges	1 t. baking powder
1/2 c. butter-flavored shortening	1/2 t. baking soda
1 c. sugar	1/2 t. salt
1/2 c. milk	2-1/2 c. powdered sugar
2 c. all-purpose flour	1 t. butter, melted

Score each orange into quarters with a sharp paring knife; peel.
Remove white pith from oranges and peels; discard pith. Quarter
oranges; add to a blender with peels. Blend until smooth; measure out
3/4 cup for use, refrigerating any remaining for use in another recipe.
Cream shortening and sugar in a large mixing bowl; blend in milk
and 6 tablespoons orange mixture. Set aside. Combine flour, baking
powder, baking soda and salt; mix into creamed mixture. Drop by
teaspoonfuls, 2 inches apart, on greased baking sheets; bake at
350 degrees for 10 to 13 minutes. Remove to wire racks to cool
completely. Whisk powdered sugar, butter and enough of the
remaining orange mixture to a desired spreading consistency; frost
cookies. Makes about 4 dozen.

*Don't pass up a trunk at
any sale. With a little paint
it not only looks like new, but
can keep magazines, toys or
holiday decorations tucked
away until needed.*

Orange Pound Cake

Juanita McLane
Wilmington, DE

I wanted to share this old Southern recipe that our family has been enjoying for over 35 years. We just love it!

1-1/2 c. butter, softened
3 c. sugar
5 eggs
3-1/2 c. all-purpose flour
1 t. cream of tartar
1-1/2 t. baking powder
1/4 t. salt

1/2 c. milk
1/2 c. plus 5 T. orange juice,
 divided
1 t. vanilla extract
1 t. almond extract
4 T. orange zest, divided
1-1/2 c. powdered sugar

Cream butter; gradually add sugar, mixing until light and fluffy. Add eggs, one at a time, blending after each addition. Combine flour, cream of tartar, baking powder and salt; add to creamed mixture alternately with the milk and 1/2 cup plus 2 tablespoons orange juice, beginning and ending with flour mixture. Mix until just blended; stir in extracts and 2 tablespoons orange zest. Pour into a greased and floured 10" Bundt® pan; bake at 325 degrees for about one hour and 25 minutes. Cool. Combine powdered sugar, remaining orange zest and enough remaining orange juice to make a desired consistency to pour over cooled cake. Serves 12.

Something as simple as a bowl filled with bingo markers or game pieces can really add whimsy to a room!

no dessert 'til you clean your plate!

Missouri Pound Cake

Amanda Saner
St. Charles, MO

Delicious plain or topped with homemade preserves.

1 c. butter, softened
3 c. sugar
6 eggs
2 T. vanilla extract

4 c. all-purpose flour
1/4 t. baking soda
1 c. sour cream

Cream butter, sugar, eggs and vanilla in a large mixing bowl; alternately add flour, baking soda and sour cream, mixing well. Divide and pour evenly into 2 greased 8"x4" loaf pans; bake at 350 degrees until a toothpick inserted in the center removes clean, about one hour. Makes 16 servings.

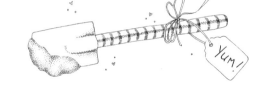

Brown Sugar Pound Cake

Kathy Grashoff
Fort Wayne, IN

A yummy spin on traditional pound cake.

1 c. butter, softened
1 c. brown sugar, packed
1 t. vanilla extract
4 eggs, beaten

1-1/2 c. plus 2 T. all-purpose flour
1-1/2 t. baking powder
1/2 t. salt

Cream butter and brown sugar until light and fluffy; mix in vanilla. Gradually blend in eggs; set aside. Combine flour, baking powder and salt; slowly blend into egg mixture. Spread batter in a lightly greased and floured 9"x5" glass loaf pan; bake at 350 degrees for 70 minutes or until a toothpick inserted in the center removes clean. Cool for one hour on a wire rack; remove from pan to cool completely. Makes 8 servings.

Apple Pie with Crumb Topping

Nancy Bigham
New Paris, OH

A recipe shared by my mother-in-law over 44 years ago. Making it brings so many happy memories.

5 c. apples, cored, peeled and
    thinly sliced
1/2 c. sugar

1 t. cinnamon
9-inch pie crust

Gently toss apples with sugar and cinnamon; arrange in the pie crust. Sprinkle with topping; bake at 350 degrees until apples are tender, about 30 to 40 minutes. Makes 8 servings.

Crumb Topping:

1/2 c. sugar
1/4 c. brown sugar, packed
1/4 c. all-purpose flour

1/4 c. wheat germ
1/4 c. butter
1/4 c. flaked coconut

Combine first 4 ingredients; cut in butter with forks or a pastry cutter until crumbly. Gently toss in coconut.

A sweet & simple gift any bride would love is a message bottle. Fill a pretty jar with antique luck charms...something old, new, borrowed and blue.

Blue Goose Pie

Jean Manahan
Waynesboro, PA

A big, berry-full slice of this pie and a scoop of vanilla ice cream is the best dessert I can imagine!

2 c. fresh gooseberries
2-1/2 c. fresh blueberries
3/4 c. sugar
1/4 t. salt

1/2 t. cinnamon
1/4 c. cornstarch
2 9-inch pie crusts
1 T. butter, sliced

In a bowl, mix together berries, sugar, salt, cinnamon and cornstarch; toss to coat berries well. Line a 9" pie plate with one pie crust. Pour berry mixture into crust; dot with butter. Cover with top crust; seal and vent crust. Bake pie at 450 degrees for 50 minutes, or until crust is golden and filling is bubbly. Serves 8.

Black-Bottom Banana Bars

Barbara Buckley
Edwards, MS

Bananas and chocolate are a terrific combination!

1/2 c. butter, softened
1 c. sugar
1 egg
1 t. vanilla extract
1-1/2 c. bananas, mashed

1-1/2 c. all-purpose flour
1 t. baking powder
1 t. baking soda
1/2 t. salt
1/4 c. baking cocoa

Cream butter and sugar; add egg and vanilla. Blend until thoroughly combined; mix in bananas. Set aside. Combine flour, baking powder, baking soda and salt; blend into banana mixture. Divide batter in half; add cocoa to one half. Pour vanilla batter into a greased 13"x9" baking pan; spoon chocolate batter on top. Swirl with a knife to make a marble appearance; bake at 350 degrees for 25 minutes. Cut into bars to serve. Makes 2-1/2 to 3 dozen.

Makin' My Own Sunshine Cake

Stacy Friend
Grand Forks, ND

As a busy mom of quadruplets, I find this easy-to-make cake a necessity when it's time for a sweet treat!

18-1/2 oz. pkg. lemon cake mix
3-oz. pkg. orange gelatin mix
1 c. boiling water

1/2 c. orange juice
8-oz. container frozen whipped
   topping, thawed

Bake cake according to package directions in a 13"x9" baking pan; set aside to cool. Poke holes over the top of the cake with a fork or skewer; set aside. Dissolve gelatin mix in water; stir in orange juice. Pour over the cake; cover and refrigerate overnight. Frost with whipped topping before serving. Makes 12 to 15 servings.

A small photo in a large frame? Give the photo a clever mat of vintage buttons...lovely!

Shoo Fly Cake

Jennifer Eveland-Kupp
Reading, PA

A little twist to an all-time favorite from Pennsylvania Dutch country.

2 c. whole-wheat flour
2 c. all-purpose flour
2 c. brown sugar, packed
1 c. butter

2 c. boiling water
1 c. molasses
2 t. baking soda

Combine flours and sugar; cut in butter with a pastry cutter until coarse crumbs form. Measure out 1-1/2 cups crumb mixture for topping; set aside. Place remaining crumb mixture in a small bowl; set aside. Blend water, molasses and baking soda together; mix in unmeasured crumb mixture, stirring until batter is thin but still lumpy. Pour into a greased and floured 13"x9" baking pan; sprinkle crumb topping mixture over the top. Bake at 350 degrees for 35 minutes. Serve warm. Makes 12 servings.

Tint new photos to look old! Just lay photos on a one-color copy machine. With dozens of colors to choose from, copies can look old instantly.

Rhubarb Robin

Robin Kittridge
Elk River, MN

Funny name, yummy dessert! Once you try it, you'll want more!

4 to 5 c. rhubarb, chopped
1 egg
1 c. sugar
3 T. all-purpose flour

18-1/2 oz. pkg. yellow cake mix
3/4 c. butter, sliced
Garnish: frozen whipped
   topping, thawed

Mash the first 4 ingredients together; pat into the bottom of an ungreased 13"x9" baking pan. Sprinkle with cake mix; arrange butter slices over the top. Do not stir. Bake at 350 degrees for 50 minutes. Cool; dollop with whipped topping before serving. Makes 12 servings.

Stumble upon a stash of old corks? Carefully cut a slit in the center to make holders for handwritten place cards!

Rhode Island Peach Slump

Betty Riser
Mount Pleasant, RI

Slump describes a cobbler-type dish topped with biscuit dough.

6 c. peaches, peeled, pitted and
    sliced
1 c. sugar
1-1/2 t. cinnamon

1/2 c. water
12 1-1/2 inch round baking
    powder biscuits
Garnish: whipping cream

Combine first 4 ingredients in a heavy skillet; bring to a boil. Reduce heat; arrange biscuits on top. Simmer, covered, for 30 minutes. Spoon into bowls; pour one or 2 tablespoons cream over the tops before serving. Makes 12 servings.

Frozen Fruitcake Dessert

Faye Davis
Owingsville, KY

Spoon into individual serving cups if you'd like.

1 c. sour cream
1/2 c. sugar
2 T. lemon juice
1 t. vanilla extract
4-1/2 oz. container frozen
    whipped topping, divided
13-oz. can crushed pineapple,
    drained

1/2 c. candied red cherries,
    chopped
1/2 c. candied green cherries,
    chopped
1/2 c. chopped walnuts

Blend first 4 ingredients and half the whipped topping together in a large mixing bowl; refrigerate remaining whipped topping for use in another recipe. Fold in remaining ingredients; spread into a 13"x9" freezer-safe pan; freeze. Serves 8 to 10.

Caramel Brownies

Harriet Ward
Chapin, SC

A cake mix makes this recipe so easy to make!

50 caramels, unwrapped
5-oz. can evaporated milk,
   divided
18-1/2 oz. pkg. German
   chocolate cake mix

1/2 c. margarine, melted
1 c. chopped nuts
1 c. chocolate chips

Place caramels and 1/3 cup evaporated milk in a microwave-safe bowl; microwave until melted, stirring often. Set aside. Combine cake mix, margarine, remaining evaporated milk and nuts. Press half the mixture into a greased 13"x9" baking pan; bake at 350 degrees for 8 minutes. Sprinkle with chocolate chips; spread caramel mixture on top. Crumble remaining cake mixture on top; bake for an additional 18 to 20 minutes. Cool; refrigerate for at least 30 minutes. Cut into squares to serve. Makes 2 to 2-1/2 dozen.

With a little soap & water and maybe a fresh coat of paint, a cast-off wooden tool caddy easily converts to countertop storage for silverware!

Cocoa-Caramel Cake

Gena Pederson
Minot, ND

This is also delicious topped with your favorite chocolate frosting recipe!

3 c. all-purpose flour
2 c. sugar
2 t. baking soda
1/4 t. salt
5 T. baking cocoa

3/4 c. oil
2 c. cold water
2 T. vinegar
2 t. vanilla extract

Combine first 5 ingredients together in a large mixing bowl; mix well and set aside. In a separate bowl, combine remaining ingredients; blend into flour mixture. Spread in a lightly greased and floured 13"x9" baking pan; bake at 350 degrees for 30 to 35 minutes. Cool; frost. Serves 12 to 15.

Caramel Frosting:

1-1/2 c. sugar
1 c. butter
1/2 c. milk

1 t. vanilla extract
1 c. nuts, chopped
Optional: 1 c. coconut

Mix first 4 ingredients together in a small saucepan; boil for 2 minutes, stirring constantly. Remove from heat; cool completely. Blend until spreadable; fold in nuts and coconut, if desired. Stir well.

Turn a 1940's kitchen cart into a rolling tote wherever the party wanders. Stocked with ice, soda and bottles of water, it's always ready with cool beverages to quench thirsts.

Cherry-Chocolate Marble Cake

Sharon Webb
Clinton, IL

Mmmm, think chocolate-covered cherries in a cake.

1 c. margarine, softened
2 c. sugar
3 eggs
6 T. maraschino cherry juice
6 T. water
2 t. almond flavoring
3-3/4 c. all-purpose flour
2-1/4 t. baking soda

3/4 t. salt
1-1/2 c. sour cream
3/4 c. maraschino cherries,
    drained and chopped
3/4 c. chopped walnuts
3 1-oz. sqs. unsweetened
    baking chocolate, melted
Garnish: powdered sugar

Cream margarine and sugar in a large mixing bowl; add eggs, one at a time, blending after each addition. Mix in cherry juice, water and almond flavoring; set aside. Combing flour, baking soda and salt; blend into creamed mixture alternately with sour cream. Place half the batter in another mixing bowl; stir in cherries and walnuts. Set aside. Blend chocolate into remaining batter; set aside. Spoon half the cherry batter into a greased 10" angel food baking pan; spoon half the chocolate batter on top. Repeat layers. Bake at 350 degrees for one hour and 15 minutes or until a toothpick inserted in the center removes clean. Cool in pan for 30 minutes; remove to a serving platter to cool completely. Sprinkle with powdered sugar before slicing. Makes 15 to 18 servings.

Gently tap old sap buckets with a rubber mallet until almost flat...a pretty wall pocket filled with flowers, dried herbs or used as a handy letter holder.

no *dessert* 'til you clean your plate!

Aunt Florence's Best-Ever Cake

Karen Davis
Columbia, SC

Growing up I loved to visit Aunt Florence. It seemed like she was always baking cookies, candy and this cake...the aromas in her house were so wonderful!

1 c. nuts
2 c. sugar
2 c. all-purpose flour
2 eggs
2 t. baking soda

15-oz. can crushed pineapple
1 t. vanilla extract
Garnish: 1/4 to 1/2 c. chopped
   nuts

Combine all ingredients; mix well. Spread in a greased 13"x9" baking pan. Bake at 350 degrees for about 40 minutes; spread with topping while warm. Sprinkle with nuts before serving. Makes 12 to 15 servings.

Topping:

1/2 c. margarine, softened
8-oz. pkg. cream cheese,
   softened

1-1/2 c. powdered sugar
1 t. vanilla extract

Cream all ingredients together until smooth and spreadable.

Weathered old feed bins make roomy containers for bushels of apples or garden tools and flowerpots.

165

Cheesecake Tarts

Mary Rita Schlagel
Warwick, NY

One word...yum!

2 8-oz. pkgs. cream cheese,
    softened
3/4 c. sugar
2 eggs
1 t. vanilla extract

1 T. lemon juice
1 t. lemon zest
18 to 20 vanilla wafer cookies
21-oz. can cherry pie filling
paper mini muffin cups

Blend first 6 ingredients together until light and fluffy, about 4 to
5 minutes; set aside. Place a vanilla wafer cookie in the bottom of
20 paper-lined mini muffin cups. Fill each 2/3 full with cream cheese
mixture; bake at 350 degrees for 20 minutes. Cool; spoon cherry pie
filling on top of each tart. Makes 20.

To whip up a pretty bed skirt in no time, just secure
colorful handkerchiefs with fusible tape and
add to a plain cotton bed skirt.

Rocky Road Fudge Brownies

Rita Miller
Wirtz, VA

Delicious warm...my husband has to eat at least 2 as soon as they come out of the oven!

1 c. butter, softened
3/4 c. baking cocoa
1/4 c. oil
4 eggs

2 c. sugar
1-1/3 c. all-purpose flour
1/2 t. salt

Combine first 3 ingredients in a small saucepan; heat until melted and smooth, stirring often. Remove from heat; set aside. Blend eggs in a large mixing bowl until light and fluffy; mix in cocoa mixture and remaining ingredients. Spread in a greased 13"x9" baking pan; bake at 350 degrees until brownies pull away from sides of pan, about 20 to 25 minutes. Sprinkle topping evenly over the top; continue baking 12 to 18 minutes. Cool; cut into bars to serve. Makes 15.

Topping:

1 c. chopped peanuts
1 c. butterscotch chips

2 c. mini marshmallows
1/2 c. chocolate ice cream syrup

Combine ingredients; mix well.

Kitchen canisters are naturals when it comes to holding beads, notions, fabric remnants and snippets of ribbon in the sewing room.

Maple Drop Cookies

Debi DeVore
Dover, OH

*Sometimes we frost with cream cheese frosting flavored with
a few drops maple flavoring.*

1 c. butter, softened
3/4 c. sugar
2 c. all-purpose flour

1/4 t. salt
1-1/2 t. maple flavoring
Optional: pecan halves

Cream butter and sugar until light and fluffy; blend in remaining
ingredients. Drop by teaspoonfuls onto greased baking sheets; place a
pecan half on top of each cookie, if desired. Bake at 350 degrees for
12 to 15 minutes. Makes about 3 dozen.

Those roomy wooden boxes that held seed packets
at the general store, are just the right size for
supplies like stationery, pens, stamps
and paper clips.

Amish Sugar Cookies

Patty Vance
Paulding, OH

During my 3 daughters' elementary school years, these cookies were served at all class events. I would get a thrill out of watching the parents send their kids up to the cookie counter for yet another one...not for the kids, but for themselves!

2 c. sugar
1 c. shortening
3 eggs
1 c. sour cream

1 t. vanilla extract
5 t. baking powder
5 c. all-purpose flour
1-1/2 t. baking soda

Cream sugar, shortening and eggs; add sour cream and vanilla. Gradually blend in remaining ingredients; mix well. Cover and refrigerate overnight. Drop by teaspoonfuls onto ungreased baking sheets; flatten slightly with the bottom of a sugar-coated glass. Bake at 350 degrees for 9 to 11 minutes; cool completely on wire racks. Frost. Makes about 4 dozen.

Frosting:

5 T. sugar
2 T. water
3 c. powdered sugar

2/3 c. shortening
1 t. vanilla extract

Add sugar and water to a small saucepan; bring to a boil. Stir and boil until sugar dissolves; remove from heat. Pour into a medium mixing bowl; set aside to cool to lukewarm. Blend in powdered sugar; mix well. Add shortening and vanilla; blending until smooth and creamy.

Keep an eye open at tag sales for metal buttons with pretty designs...they make such clever wax stamps for cards and letters.

Giant Chocolate Malt Cookies

Pat Habiger
Spearville, KS

The next best thing to a good old-fashioned malted shake!

1 c. butter-flavored shortening	2 c. all-purpose flour
1-1/4 c. brown sugar, packed	1 t. baking soda
1/2 c. malted milk powder	1/2 t. salt
2 T. chocolate syrup	1-1/2 c. semi-sweet chocolate
1 T. vanilla extract	chunks
1 egg	1 c. milk chocolate chips

Combine first 5 ingredients in a large mixing bowl; blend for 2 minutes. Add egg; blend well and set aside. Mix flour, baking soda and salt together; gradually blend into the creamed mixture. Fold in chocolates; shape dough into 2-inch balls. Arrange 3 inches apart on ungreased baking sheets; bake at 375 degrees for 12 to 14 minutes. Cool for 2 minutes before removing to a wire rack to cool completely. Makes 1-1/2 dozen.

A popcorn chenille bedspread would make a fun shower curtain!

Spicy Oatmeal-Raisin Cookies

Terri Childress
Staunton, VA

Try sweetened dried cranberries for a brand new taste.

18-1/2 oz. pkg. spice cake mix
2 c. quick-cooking oats,
    uncooked
2 eggs
1/2 c. oil
1/2 c. milk
1-1/2 to 2 c. raisins
1/4 c. brown sugar, packed
Optional: 1 c. chopped nuts

Combine ingredients; mix well. Drop by tablespoonfuls onto ungreased baking sheets; bake at 350 degrees for 13 to 15 minutes. Remove to wire cooling rack immediately. Makes about 4 dozen.

Grandma's Teacakes

Karen Ahern
Rehoboth, MA

I was always running next door to see Grandma when she made cookies and cakes. Knowing I just loved this cake, she shared this treasured recipe with me.

1 c. butter, softened
1 c. powdered sugar, divided
2-1/4 c. all-purpose flour
1/4 t. salt
1 t. vanilla extract
3/4 c. ground walnuts

Cream butter and 1/2 cup powdered sugar together; mix in flour. Add salt and vanilla; mix well. Blend in walnuts; form into walnut-size balls. Arrange on ungreased baking sheets; bake at 325 degrees for 14 to 17 minutes. Roll in remaining powdered sugar to coat; set aside to cool. Roll again in powdered sugar; store in an airtight container. Makes 2 dozen.

Banana-Chocolate Chip Cookies

Charlotte Russell
Cambridge, NY

What else can I say? These are great!

1/2 c. sugar
1 egg
1/3 c. shortening
1/2 c. bananas, mashed
1 c. all-purpose flour
1/4 t. salt

1 t. baking powder
1/2 t. baking soda
1/2 t. vanilla extract
1 c. semi-sweet
   chocolate chips
Optional: 1/2 c. chopped nuts

Blend sugar, egg and shortening together; mix in bananas. Add flour, salt, baking powder, baking soda and vanilla; mix well. Fold in chocolate chips and nuts, if desired. Drop by spoonfuls onto greased baking sheets; bake at 375 degrees for 12 to 15 minutes. Makes about 4 dozen.

Glass apothecary and barbershop jars can spiff up the powder room in lots of ways by holding cotton balls, bath-oil beads or miniature soaps.

no *dessert* 'til you clean your plate!

Soft Gingerbread Cookies

Bev Johnstone
Delaware, OH

My mother always made these cookies at Christmastime when I was a little girl. I carried on the tradition for my children and now make them for my grandson. They are so soft and moist...a true favorite.

1 c. margarine
1-1/2 c. brown sugar, packed
2 eggs, beaten
1 T. ground ginger
1/2 c. molasses
1-1/2 c. boiling water

1-1/2 t. baking soda
5 c. all-purpose flour
2 t. baking powder
1-1/2 t. salt
1 T. cinnamon
1 c. chopped walnuts

Cream margarine and sugar in a large mixing bowl; blend in eggs. Mix in ginger and molasses; stir in boiling water. Set aside. Combine remaining ingredients except for the nuts; add to sugar mixture. Fold in walnuts; cover and refrigerate dough for at least 2 hours. Drop by teaspoonfuls onto ungreased baking sheets; bake at 425 degrees for 10 to 12 minutes. Makes about 6 dozen.

Pint-size Victorian garden urns are one item to snap up at any flea market! Whether they hold hand towels in the guest room, lemons in the kitchen or bouquets of flowers, they seem to make everything more elegant.

Oatmeal Sweets

Kim Johnson
Abilene, KS

When I was young girl, I couldn't wait to go to Ada's house because I knew what kind of treat I was going to get...this yummy oatmeal candy!

2 c. sugar
1/2 c. milk
1/2 c. margarine

3/4 c. creamy peanut butter
3 c. quick-cooking oats,
    uncooked

Combine sugar, milk and margarine in a heavy saucepan; bring to a boil. Stir and boil for 2 minutes; remove from heat. Stir in peanut butter and oats; mix well. Drop by teaspoonfuls onto wax paper; set aside until firm. Makes about 1-1/2 pounds.

Beaded flowers and fruits bring a smile to almost anyone's face. Tuck a single beaded flower in a bouquet or a beaded pear or banana alongside the fruit in a fruit bowl for a whimsical surprise.

Peanut Butter Tassies

Cherie White
Oklahoma City, OK

Makes 24 of the most delicious peanut butter cups.

1/2 c. butter, softened
3-oz. pkg. cream cheese,
   softened
1 c. all-purpose flour
1 egg

1/4 t. vanilla extract
1/4 t. lemon juice concentrate
1/2 c. sugar
1 c. peanut butter chips, chopped

Combine butter, cream cheese and flour together; refrigerate for one hour. Roll into 24 one-inch balls; place balls into greased mini muffin cups. Press dough up the sides and on the bottom of each mini muffin cup; set aside. Combine remaining ingredients; fill each dough cup 3/4 full. Bake at 350 degrees for 20 minutes or until firm. Makes 2 dozen.

Corn Flake Chews

Jeanne Rash
Woodside, DE

Makes a tasty after-school snack.

1 c. corn syrup
1 c. sugar
1 c. creamy peanut butter

1 T. butter
6 c. corn flake cereal

Bring first 2 ingredients to a boil, then stir in next 2 ingredients. Stir until melted; pour over corn flake cereal. Spread and lightly press into a buttered 13"x9" pan; set aside to cool. Cut into bars to serve. Makes 2 dozen.

All-American Trifle

Lisa Mayfield
Branchburg, NJ

Bursting with berries!

18-1/2 oz. pkg. white cake mix
1 qt. strawberries, hulled, sliced
   in half and divided
1 pt. blueberries, divided
1 pt. raspberries, divided

1 pt. blackberries, divided
raspberry liqueur or ice cream
   syrup
16-oz. container frozen whipped
   topping, thawed and divided

Prepare cake according to package directions; pour into a greased 9"x9" baking pan. Bake as directed; cool. Cut into one-inch squares; arrange one layer in a trifle bowl; scatter a layer of strawberry slices between the cake squares. Top with a layer of blueberries, raspberries and blackberries; drizzle raspberry liqueur or syrup over the top. Spread with a thin layer whipped topping; repeat layers until no more cake remains. Chill until ready to serve. Serves 15.

Simple wooden shelves are a flea market standby and with very little effort, they easily become charming display cases for favorite collections.

Lemonade Pie

Anna Nahajewski
Lexington, SC

I love to serve this in the summertime...so refreshing.

14-oz. can sweetened condensed
   milk
6-oz. can frozen lemonade
   concentrate, partially thawed

4 drops yellow food coloring
8-oz. container frozen whipped
   topping, thawed
9-inch graham cracker pie crust

Combine milk, lemonade and food coloring; fold in whipped topping,
mixing well. Spoon into pie crust; freeze. Remove from freezer
15 minutes before serving. Makes 8 servings.

Watermelon Sorbet Pie

Elaine Nichols
Mesa, AZ

Try using chocolate chunks for a big chocolate flavor!

2 pts. raspberry sorbet, softened
1 c. mini semi-sweet chocolate
   chips
9-inch graham cracker pie crust

2 pts. lemon sorbet, softened
   and divided
10 to 15 drops green food
   coloring

Combine raspberry sorbet and chocolate chips; spoon into pie crust.
Freeze for one hour; smooth 1-1/4 cup lemon sorbet over the top.
Freeze for an additional hour; set aside. Mix remaining lemon sorbet
with food coloring; spread on top of frozen pie. Freeze for at least one
additional hour. Makes 8 servings.

Southern Biscuit Shortcakes

Linda Stone
Cookeville, TN

Shortcake southern style!

6 c. strawberries, hulled and
   sliced
sugar to taste
2 c. self-rising flour

3 T. sugar, divided
1/2 c. chilled butter, sliced
3/4 c. half-and-half
1 c. whipping cream

Combine strawberries with sugar in a mixing bowl; cover with plastic wrap and refrigerate. Mix flour and 2 tablespoons sugar together; cut in butter with a pastry blender until coarse crumbs form. Add half-and-half; stir until just moistened. Knead dough on a lightly floured surface until smooth; roll out to 1/2-inch thickness. Cut out with a floured 3-inch round biscuit cutter; arrange on a greased baking sheet. Bake at 450 degrees until golden, about 9 to 12 minutes. Remove to a wire rack to cool to lukewarm; set aside. Blend whipping cream with remaining sugar until stiff peaks form; set aside. Split shortcakes in half horizontally with a serrated knife; place bottom half on a serving plate and cover with chilled sweetened strawberries. Replace top half; add a dollop of whipped cream. Makes one dozen.

Don't forget about thrift shops and yard sales...they can be sources for some of the best vintage finds!

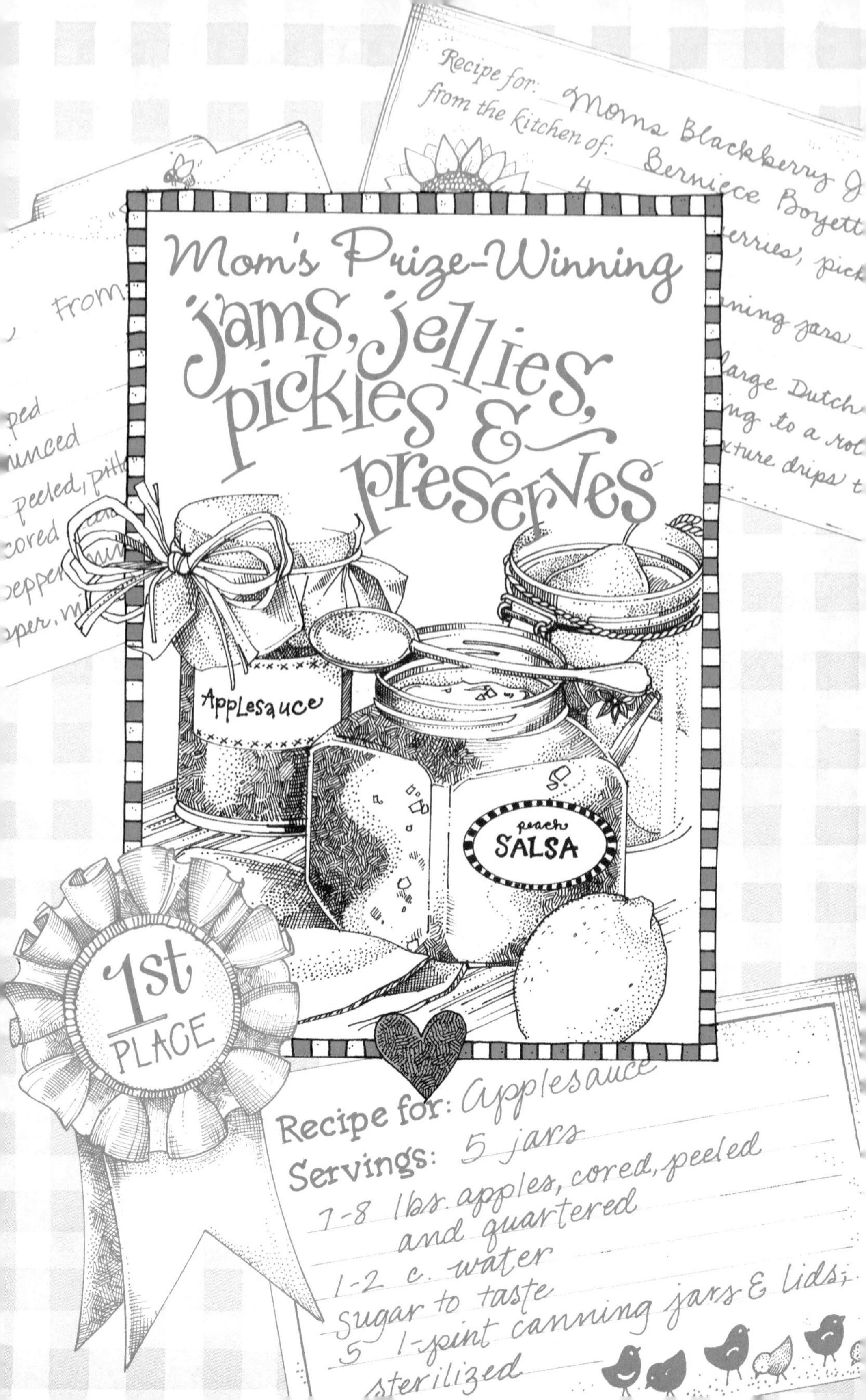

From

ped
unced
peeled, pitt
cored
pepper
per, m

Mom's Prize-Winning
Jams, jellies, pickles & preserves

Applesauce

peach SALSA

1st PLACE

Recipe for: Applesauce
Servings: 5 jars
7-8 lbs. apples, cored, peeled
and quartered
1-2 c. water
sugar to taste
5 1-pint canning jars & lids,
sterilized

Great Basics for Everyday Canning

Wondering how much water should be in a boiling water bath? Add enough to cover the canning jars by one to 2 inches. Also, the water in the pot should remain one to 2 inches below the rim when boiling and with jars submerged.

Old canning jars with zinc lids are beautiful for gift-giving, but not long-term storage. Use them only for preserves being stored in the refrigerator.

It's easy to sterilize jars and lids...just submerge them in water, bring to a boil, reduce heat and allow to simmer for 10 minutes. Turn off heat, but don't remove jars and lids from hot water until ready to fill and use.

Don't forget when placing jars in a boiling water bath, the jars should be placed about one inch apart from each other so they're not touching.

A slight indentation in the lid indicates a vacuum seal; the lid should not flex up and down when pressed firmly with a finger. Remember to keep canned goodies in a cool, dry, dark place to enjoy for up to one year.

Wondering what headspace is and why it's different on some recipes? Headspace is simply the space between the food inside the jar and the top of the jar. Always use the recommended headspace given in each recipe...too much headspace will cause the jar not to seal, too little will cause the contents to overflow.

Mom's Blackberry Jam

Berniece Boyett
Rogers, AR

As a child, growing up on a farm in Illinois, I helped pick the berries for this delicious jam. My mother and I would rise early while the grass was still heavy with dew and go to the berry patch in a nearby pasture.

4 c. blackberries, washed and hulled
4 c. sugar

4 1/2-pint canning jars and lids, sterilized

Place blackberries in a large Dutch oven; just cover with water. Bring to a rolling boil; add sugar. Boil until mixture drips thickly from a wooden spoon, about 30 to 45 minutes. Spoon into hot sterilized jars, leaving 1/4-inch headspace. Wipe rims; secure with lids and rings. Process in a boiling water bath for 10 minutes; set jars on a towel to cool. Check for seals. Makes 4 jars.

Happiness is like jam. You can't spread even a little without getting some on yourself!

– Unknown

Pumpkin Butter

Bonnie Zeilenga
DeMotte, IN

When Fall rolls along, it's time for this spicy, sweet recipe.

29-oz. can pumpkin purée
3/4 c. apple juice
2 t. ground ginger
1/2 t. ground cloves
1-1/2 c. sugar

2 t. cinnamon
1 t. nutmeg
5 1/2-pint canning jars and lids,
  sterilized

Combine ingredients in a large heavy saucepan; stir well. Bring mixture to a boil; reduce heat and simmer until thickened, about 30 minutes, stirring frequently. Spoon into hot sterilized jars, leaving 1/4-inch headspace. Wipe rims; secure with lids and rings. Process in a boiling water bath for 10 minutes; set jars on a towel to cool. Check for seals. Makes 5 jars.

When visiting the pumpkin patch, pick up several small sugar pumpkins. Hollowed out, they're just the right size for tucking a 1/2-pint jar of Pumpkin Butter into. Tie a spreader to the stem handle with raffia for a gift anyone will love!

Colonial Apple Butter

Kathy Grashoff
Fort Wayne, IN

So easy to prepare, get together with the family to make this old-fashioned recipe.

4-1/2 c. apple cider
14 c. apples, cored, peeled and
    chopped
1/2 c. maple syrup
1 t. cinnamon

1/2 t. ground cloves
1/2 t. allspice
3 1-pint canning jars and lids,
    sterilized

Pour cider into a large Dutch oven; boil for 15 minutes. Stir in apples; reduce heat. Cover and simmer until tender, about one hour; stir every 15 minutes. Remove from heat; mash apples with a potato masher. Add remaining ingredients; return to low heat. Heat, uncovered, and stir until thickened, about 30 minutes; remove from heat. Set aside for 15 minutes. Spoon into hot sterilized jars, leaving 1/4-inch headspace. Wipe rims; secure with lids and rings. Process in a boiling water bath for 10 minutes; set jars on a towel to cool. Check for seals. Makes 3 jars.

For an extra-special touch, use vines of bittersweet or rosehips to make a wreath and slip around jars of Colonial Apple Butter. Pretty enough for gift-giving or lined up on a cupboard shelf as an Autumn display.

Red Raspberry Jam

Jo Ann

*Tempting to eat before they're even made into jam,
raspberries are an all-time favorite!*

4 c. red raspberries, hulled
1-3/4 oz. pkg. powdered pectin
2 T. lemon juice
6-1/2 c. sugar
5 1/2-pint canning jars and
   lids, sterilized

Lightly crush raspberries in a large heavy stockpot; heat over high
heat. Add pectin and lemon juice; bring to a boil, stirring constantly.
Gradually add sugar, stirring until dissolved; return mixture to a boil.
Boil for one minute; remove from heat. Spoon into hot sterilized jars,
leaving 1/4-inch headspace. Wipe rims; secure with lids and rings.
Process in a boiling water bath for 10 minutes; set jars on a towel to
cool. Check for seals. Makes 5 jars.

Terra cotta pots are found everywhere at
summertime sales. Ideal timing for Red
Raspberry Jam gifts! Tuck a jar inside the pot
and top it off with a matching saucer for the lid.
Just turn the saucer upside down. For added
security, tape the saucer in place and add a
ribbon to cover the tape; top with a big bow.

Mom's Prize-Winning Jams, Jellies, Pickles & Preserves

Homemade Strawberry Jam

Carol Burns
Delaware, OH

Our family's favorite jam...we also heat up and pour over ice cream.

5 c. strawberries, hulled and
   crushed
1-3/4 oz. pkg. powdered pectin

7 c. sugar
8 1/2-pint canning jars and lids,
   sterilized

Combine strawberries and pectin in an 8-quart heavy saucepan; bring to a rolling boil over high heat, stirring constantly. Mix in sugar; return to rolling boil and boil for one minute. Skim off any foam using a metal spoon; discard. Ladle into jars, leaving 1/8-inch headspace; wipe rims and secure lids. Process in a boiling water bath for 10 minutes; set jars on a towel to cool. Check for seals. Makes 8 jars.

Strawberry Freezer Jam

Connie Bryant
Topeka, KS

Freezer jams are a snap to make and taste amazing!

2 c. strawberries, hulled and
   crushed
4 c. sugar
1-3/4 oz. pkg. powdered pectin

3/4 c. water
5 1/2-pint freezer-safe airtight
   plastic containers, sterilized

Combine strawberries and sugar in a large mixing bowl; set aside. Whisk pectin and water together in a small saucepan; bring to a boil. Boil and stir for one minute; remove from heat. Pour pectin mixture over fruit and sugar; stir until sugar dissolves, about 3 minutes. Spoon into containers leaving 1/2-inch headspace; secure lids. Set aside at room temperature until set, up to 24 hours. Freeze up to one year. Makes 5 containers.

Slow-Cooker Apricot Preserves

Tina Stidam
Delaware, OH

For a short cut, just spoon into airtight, freezer-proof containers after jam has thickened and keep stored in the freezer up to 3 months.

1-lb. pkg. dried apricots
1-3/4 c. sugar
3-1/2 c. water

4 1/2-pint canning jars and lids, sterilized

Finely chop apricots in a food processor; place in a slow cooker. Stir in sugar and water; cover and heat on high setting for 2-1/2 hours, stirring twice. Uncover and continue heating on high setting until thickened, about 2 hours; stir occasionally. Spoon into hot sterilized jars, leaving 1/4-inch headspace. Wipe rims; secure with lids and rings. Process in a boiling water bath for 10 to 15 minutes; set jars on a towel to cool. Check for seals. Makes 4 jars.

Apricot Preserves make a delicious addition to rice at dinnertime. Just add 2 tablespoons of preserves along with the water when preparing rice. Stir in one teaspoon curry powder, 1/4 cup slivered almonds and 1/4 cup raisins; prepare as directed.

Mom's Prize-Winning Jams, Jellies, Pickles & Preserves

Pear Honey

Ann Rennier
Columbia, MO

Handed down for generations, this recipe is a favorite spooned on homemade bread or biscuits.

8 lbs. pears, cored and peeled
6 lbs. sugar
1 T. butter

20-oz. can crushed pineapple
10 to 12 1/2-pint canning jars
  and lids, sterilized

Grate pears; place in a large heavy saucepan. Add sugar and butter; mix well. Bring to a boil; boil gently for 2 hours. Stir in pineapple; boil another 5 minutes. Spoon into hot sterilized jars, leaving 1/4-inch headspace. Wipe rims; secure with lids and rings. Process in a boiling water bath for 10 minutes; set jars on a towel to cool. Check for seals. Makes 10 to 12 jars.

Slow-Cooker Peach Spread

Sally Junkins
Mount Pleasant, SC

Let the slow cooker do all the work!

4 30-oz. cans peaches, drained
3 to 4 c. sugar
2 t. cinnamon
1 t. ground cloves

2 T. lemon juice
4 1/2-pint canning jars and lids,
  sterilized

Purée peaches; place in a slow cooker. Add remaining ingredients; cover and heat on high setting for 8 to 10 hours, removing cover for last 4 hours. Stir occasionally. Spoon into hot sterilized jars, leaving 1/4-inch headspace. Wipe rims; secure with lids and rings. Process in a boiling water bath for 10 minutes; set jars on a towel to cool. Check for seals. Makes 4 jars.

Gooseberry Jam

Donna May
Greensburg, KY

Making jams and jellies with Grandma are my most
cherished childhood memories.

4 qts. gooseberries, hulled and
    rinsed
3 lbs. sugar

8 1-pint canning jars and lids,
    sterilized

Place gooseberries in a large mixing bowl; pour sugar on top. Cover
and set aside overnight. Pour into a large stockpot; heat over medium
heat, stirring until boiling. Gently mash with a potato masher; heat
until mixture thickens, stirring often. Spoon into hot sterilized jars,
leaving 1/4-inch headspace. Wipe rims; secure with lids and rings.
Process in a boiling water bath for 15 minutes; set jars on a towel to
cool. Check for seals. Makes 8 jars.

When giving sweet preserves, don't forget to add
a loaf of homemade bread or muffins and creamy
butter so they can be enjoyed right away!

Blueberry Chutney

Gaylee Bork
Lacona, NY

A unique combination of ingredients make a tasty spread!

2 apples, cored, peeled and
   chopped
1 onion, chopped
3 t. dried basil
1 c. vinegar

1 c. brown sugar, packed
1 qt. blueberries
6 1/2-pint canning jars and lids,
   sterilized

Combine apples, onion and basil in a 4-quart saucepan; add vinegar and brown sugar. Heat on low heat; stir in blueberries. Bring to a boil; reduce heat and simmer for 20 to 30 minutes. Spoon into hot sterilized jars, leaving 1/4-inch headspace. Wipe rims; secure with lids and rings. Process in a boiling water bath for 10 minutes; set jars on a towel to cool. Check for seals. Makes 6 jars.

Cranberry Chutney

Calla Andrews
Long Beach, CA

So good, we eat it with everything!

16-oz. pkg. cranberries
2 c. sugar
1 c. water
1 T. orange zest
1 c. orange juice
1 c. raisins

1 c. celery, diced
1 apple, cored, peeled and
   minced
1 T. whole ginger, minced
6 1/2-pint canning jars and lids,
   sterilized

Bring cranberries, sugar and water to a boil in heavy 3-quart saucepan, stirring often; reduce heat and simmer 15 minutes. Stir in remaining ingredients; remove from heat. Ladle into sterilized jars; secure with lids. Refrigerate up to 3 weeks. Makes 6 jars.

Strawberry-Jalapeño Sauce

Kory Hagler
Bismarck, ND

Drizzle this over softened cream cheese and serve with crackers for a yummy appetizer or use as a marinade for chicken.

3-1/2 c. strawberries, crushed
1 c. jalapeños, minced
1-3/4 oz. pkg. powdered pectin
1/2 t. margarine
3 T. lemon juice

4 c. sugar
1 c. corn syrup
8 1/2-pint canning jars and lids,
   sterilized

Combine strawberries and jalapeños in a 6-quart saucepan; stir in pectin, margarine and lemon juice. Bring to a rolling boil over high heat, stirring constantly; add sugar and corn syrup. Return to a rolling boil; boil for one minute, stirring constantly. Remove from heat; skim and discard any foam. Fill sterilized canning jars, leaving 1/8-inch headspace; wipe rims. Secure with sterilized lids and rings. Process in a boiling water bath for 10 minutes; set jars on a towel to cool. Check for seals. Makes 8 jars.

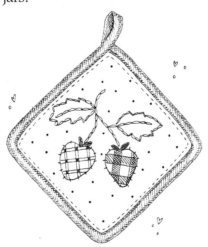

Don't fret if your jellies don't set...they'll make amazing fruit syrups for breakfast or for spooning over ice cream!

Peach Salsa

Kristine Marumoto
Sandy, UT

Quite a tasty spin on the "usual" salsa recipes.

20 tomatoes, chopped
6 onions, minced
5 peaches, peeled, pitted and
   chopped
5 pears, cored, peeled and
   chopped
1 green pepper, minced

1 red pepper, minced
4 c. sugar
2 T. canning salt
1/4 c. pickling spice, wrapped
   and tied in cheesecloth
8 1-pint canning jars and lids,
   sterilized

Bring all ingredients to a boil in a large, heavy stockpot; reduce heat and simmer until sauce is reduced by half, about 1-1/2 hours. Stir occasionally; remove spice bag. Spoon into sterilized jars; secure with lids and rings. Set aside to cool. Refrigerate up to 2 weeks. Makes 8 jars.

For clever jar toppers use vintage ribbons, tags, quilt squares or something as simple as a newspaper between the sealed lid and ring of a filled canning jar.

Aunt Ceil's Refrigerated Pickles

Mary Ann Nemecek
Springfield, IL

Aunt Ceil owned and operated her own homestyle restaurant. One summer many years ago she gave us a jar of these delicious pickles along with the recipe. We were amazed at how easy it was to make them and have shared the recipe with many family & friends.

1 gal. cucumbers, sliced
3 onions, thinly sliced
1 gal. glass jar with lid
1 T. mustard seed
2 T. celery seed

1 t. turmeric
3 c. white vinegar
3 c. sugar
1/3 c. canning salt

Layer cucumbers and onions in the glass jar; set aside. Whisk remaining ingredients together; pour over cucumbers and onions. Secure lid; refrigerate. Shake twice a day for the next 7 days. Keep refrigerated. Makes one gallon.

Sweet Freezer Pickles

Brad Daugherty
Columbus, OH

An amazingly easy recipe!

4 c. cucumbers, thinly sliced
2 c. onions, thinly sliced
4 t. salt without iodine
2 T. water
3/4 c. sugar

1/2 c. cider vinegar
1 t. dill weed
4 1/2-pint freezer-safe airtight
    plastic containers, sterilized

Combine first 4 ingredients in a large mixing bowl; let stand 2 hours. Drain; do not rinse. Stir in remaining ingredients. Set aside; stir occasionally until sugar dissolves and liquid covers vegetables. Pack in containers leaving a one-inch headspace; secure lids. Freeze. Thaw at room temperature to serve. Makes 4 containers.

Mom's Prize-Winning Jams, Jellies, pickles & preserves

Crispy Sweet Pickles

Ann Brown
Winnsboro, TX

*A wonderful recipe found in my mother's 50-year-old cookbook.
If you can't find slaked lime at your grocery, look for pickling
lime...it's the same ingredient with a different name.*

7 lbs. cucumbers, sliced
2 gal. water
2 c. slaked lime
2 qts. white vinegar
4-1/2 lbs. sugar
3 T. canning salt

1 t. celery seed
1 t. whole cloves
1 t. mixed pickling spice
3-inch cinnamon stick
14 1-pint canning jars and lids,
    sterilized

Combine the first 3 ingredients in a large mixing bowl; cover and set
aside for 24 hours, stirring occasionally. Drain and rinse until the
water runs clear; soak cucumbers in ice water for 3 hours. Drain. Mix
the remaining ingredients together; pour over cucumbers. Let stand
overnight. Pour cucumber mixture into a large stockpot; bring to a boil.
Reduce heat and simmer for 35 minutes; stir often. Pack in
sterilized jars; wipe rims. Secure lids and rings; process in a boiling
water bath for 10 minutes. Set jars on a towel to cool; check for seals.
Makes 14 jars.

*Have friends, not for the sake of receiving,
but of giving.*

– Joseph Roux

Salsa for a Year

Jennifer Licon-Conner
Gooseberry Patch

Have fun and plant a salsa garden! Add rows of tomatoes, jalapeños, onions and garlic to your garden; it's so easy and tastes so fresh.

15 lbs. roma tomatoes, cored, peeled and chopped
2-1/4 lbs. jalapeños, chopped
3 lbs. onions, chopped
2 c. cider vinegar
3 T. plus 1 t. canning salt

25 cloves garlic, peeled and chopped
1/2 c. sweet paprika
15 1-pint canning jars and lids, sterilized

Combine all ingredients in a 5-gallon stockpot; stir well. Heat to a boil, stirring often; reduce heat and simmer for 10 minutes. Spoon into jars, leaving 1/2-inch headspace; wipe rims. Secure lids; process in a boiling water bath for 15 minutes. Set jars on a towel to cool for 24 hours; check for seals. Makes 15 jars.

Jars of salsa and chips make an ideal party appetizer, why not tote them along in a Southwestern-style basket? Line the basket with festive bandannas, create jar labels and toppers using colorful beads and fabrics, then tuck in bags of tortilla chips. So simple!

Red Pepper Jam

Stephanie Christman
Keno, OR

A great dip for chips, crackers or spread on hamburgers.

12 red peppers	2 c. cider vinegar
1 T. canning salt	5 1/2-pint canning jars and lids,
3 c. sugar	sterilized

Remove and discard stems and seeds from peppers; grind in a food processor. Mix in salt; cover and refrigerate for 12 hours. Drain and discard juice; place remaining mixture in a large stockpot. Stir in sugar and vinegar; heat over medium heat for 45 minutes, stirring often. Pour into sterilized jars; wipe rims. Secure lids and rings; process in a boiling water bath for 10 minutes. Set jars on a towel to cool; check for seals. Makes 5 jars.

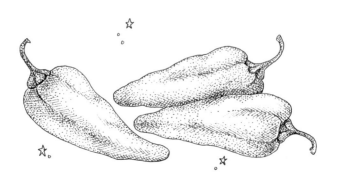

Whip up a picnic gift basket in minutes! Fill a retro picnic tin with savory jams...perfect as sandwich spreads or dips for veggies and bread sticks.

Norma's BBQ Sauce

Nancy Price
Dublin, OH

*My mother, Norma, was head cook in the Pine Street Cafe in the
1950's and she's shared this favorite recipe with me.*

6 c. onion, chopped
3 c. margarine
12-oz. pkg. all-purpose flour
6 c. vinegar
1/4 c. hot pepper sauce
4 qts. water
1-1/4 c. Worcestershire sauce

2-1/2 t. pepper
8 qts. catsup
1 c. chili powder
1-1/2 lbs. brown sugar
1 c. mustard
13 1-quart catsup bottles and
   lids, sterilized

Heat onions with margarine slightly; whisk in flour. Heat until onions
are tender; place in a very large stockpot. Add remaining ingredients;
heat until boiling. Pour into sterilized catsup bottles; wipe rims. Secure
with sterilized lids; set aside to cool to room temperature. May keep in
the freezer up to one year; thaw to use. Makes 13 bottles.

*Canning is more fun assembly-line style with a
group of friends sharing the process and the
yummy rewards!*

All-Pasta Sauce
Vickie

Use in place of tomato or spaghetti sauce all year long.

8 qts. tomatoes, chopped
2 green peppers, chopped
1-1/2 lbs. onions, chopped
2 cloves garlic, chopped
1 c. oil
1/4 c. canning salt
1/2 T. dried oregano

1-1/2 T. dried basil
1 T. dried parsley
3/4 c. sugar
24-oz. can tomato paste
2 bay leaves
6 1-quart canning jars and lids,
   sterilized

Grind tomatoes, green peppers and onions in batches in a blender; add to a large stockpot. Bring to a boil; boil gently for one hour. Stir in remaining ingredients; boil one hour longer. Remove bay leaves. Spoon into hot sterilized jars, leaving 1/2-inch headspace. Wipe rims; secure with lids and rings. Process in a boiling water bath for 20 minutes; set jars on a towel to cool. Check for seals. Makes 6 jars.

Pasta dishes are an all-time favorite, so be sure to have plenty of napkins on hand! For clever napkin rings, punch a hole in the center of each of the long sides on a button card. Slide ribbon through the holes, slip the napkin through and tighten ribbon to secure the napkin.

Mom's Pickled Beets

Teresa Beal
Delaware, OH

Grandma's recipe was handed down to my Aunt, then shared with me. All the grandchildren agree that no holiday meal is complete without these pickled beets!

4 lbs. beets
1 qt. vinegar
1-1/2 c. water
1 c. sugar
1-1/2 t. canning salt

3 T. mixed whole pickling
   spices, tied in cheesecloth
4 1-pint canning jars and lids,
   sterilized

Boil beets until tender, about 45 to 55 minutes; slice 1/2 inch off the tops and discard. Place beets under cold water; peel, slice and set aside. Place remaining ingredients in a heavy saucepan: bring to a boil and boil 5 minutes. Fill jars with beet slices; add liquid, leaving 1/2-inch headspace. Wipe rims; secure lids and rings. Process in a boiling water bath for 30 minutes; set jars on a towel to cool. Check for seals. Makes 4 jars.

Fill a wire milk-bottle carrier with a variety of canned jams, jellies and salsas...an easy way to tote them to any get-together!

The Best-Ever Tomatoes

April Jacobs
Loveland, CO

Enjoy a wonderful fresh-from-the-garden taste by adding these to your favorite chili recipe.

15 lbs. tomatoes
boiling water
14 T. lemon juice, divided or
   3-1/2 t. citric acid, divided

7 t. canning salt, divided
7 1-quart canning jars and lids,
   sterilized

Dip tomatoes into boiling water until skins split, about 30 to 60 seconds; plunge under cold water and peel. Core; cut into half, if desired. Set aside. Add 2 tablespoons lemon juice or 1/2 teaspoon citric acid to each jar; add tomatoes. Cover with hot water, leaving 1/2-inch headspace; add one teaspoon salt to each jar. Remove air bubbles; secure lids. Process in a boiling water bath for 45 minutes; set jars on a towel to cool. Check for seals. Makes 7 jars.

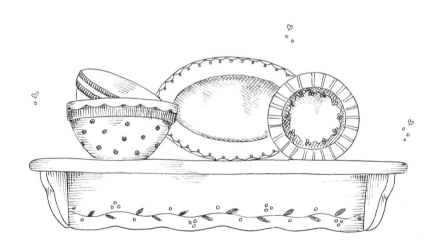

For a clever jar topper on The Best-Ever Tomatoes, use a length of jute to secure on a bundle of fresh basil leaves...so fragrant!

Zucchini Relish

Mary Dungan
Gardenville, PA

Use anywhere you like pickle relish...hot dogs, hamburgers or coneys.

10 c. zucchini, chopped
4 c. onions, chopped
4 c. red peppers, chopped
4-oz. can diced green chiles
3 T. canning salt
3-1/2 c. sugar
3 c. cider vinegar

1 T. turmeric
4 t. celery seed
1 t. pepper
1/2 t. nutmeg
5 1-pint canning jars and lids,
  sterilized

Combine zucchini, onions, red peppers, chiles and salt in a large mixing bowl; stir well. Cover and refrigerate overnight. Rinse and drain; set aside. Mix remaining ingredients in a large stockpot; bring to a boil. Add zucchini mixture; simmer for 10 minutes. Spoon into sterilized jars, leaving 1/4-inch headspace; wipe rims. Secure with sterilized lids and rings; process for 10 minutes in a boiling water bath. Set jars on a wire rack to cool to room temperature. Check for seals. Makes 5 jars.

Use a few strands of raffia to secure a pretty silver serving spoon to a jar of Zucchini Relish. The spoon will be a constant reminder of a tasty and thoughtful gift!

Gingerberry Relish

Elizabeth Blackstone
Racine, WI

Serve warm with a turkey dinner or chilled and spread on turkey sandwiches…anywhere you'd use cranberry sauce.

8-1/4 oz. can crushed pineapple
2/3 c. sugar
3/4 t. ground ginger
1/2 c. water
12-oz. pkg. cranberries
Garnish: 1/2 c. chopped walnuts

Combine undrained pineapple, sugar, ginger and water in a medium saucepan; heat until sugar dissolves, stirring frequently. Add cranberries; bring to a boil. Reduce heat; simmer until cranberries pop, about 3 to 4 minutes. Transfer to an airtight container. Keep refrigerated up to 3 days. Garnish with walnuts before serving. Makes 10 to 12 servings.

Gooseberry Relish

Sherry Gordon
Arlington Heights, IL

A tasty side with a favorite pork roast dinner.

5 c. gooseberries, chopped
1 c. brown sugar, packed
1-1/2 c. raisins, chopped
1 onion, peeled and chopped
3 T. salt
1/4 t. cayenne pepper
1 t. mustard
1 t. ground ginger
1 t. turmeric
1 qt. vinegar

Combine ingredients in a large, heavy stockpot; heat to boiling. Reduce heat and simmer for 45 minutes; stir often. Rub through a coarse sieve; store in an airtight container in the refrigerator. Warm through before serving. Makes 6 to 7 servings.

Applesauce

Jennifer Dutcher
Lewis Center, OH

Everyone loves applesauce...try sprinkling it with a little cinnamon before serving.

7 to 8 lbs. apples, cored, peeled
    and quartered
1 to 2 c. water

sugar
5 1-pint canning jars and lids,
    sterilized

Place apples in a large stockpot; add one to 2 cups water. Simmer, covered, until tender; remove from heat. Press apples through a food mill or coarse sieve; place apple mixture back into stockpot. Add sugar to taste; bring to a boil. Remove from heat; spoon into jars, leaving 1/2-inch headspace. Remove air bubbles; secure lids. Process in a boiling water bath for 20 minutes. Set aside to cool to room temperature; check for seals. Makes 5 jars.

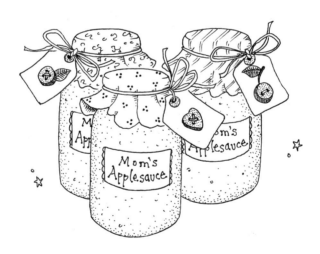

Fill an orchard basket with crunchy apples, caramel dip, spiced apple tea, warm biscuits and jars of homemade applesauce...a fall gift bursting with the best of the season!

Use it up,
wear it out,
make it do
or do without...

Clever uses
for flea-
market finds

Cream PIONEER Soda

BLACK CHERRY SODA

Quality Wash & Iron

Gelatin Mold Candle

Because old-fashioned molds come in such terrific shapes, they make the best candle molds!

clear candle wax
empty coffee can
saucepan
awl
gelatin mold

bowl
birthday candles
jelly beans, gummies, gumdrops
or conversation hearts

Break wax into several small pieces and place in coffee can. Place the coffee can in a saucepan large enough to hold it; fill pan 2/3 with water. Heat over medium-low heat until wax has melted. Use an awl to make a small hole in the top center of the gelatin mold. Place the mold, bottom-side up, into a bowl. Put the birthday candle, upside down, into the mold, slipping the wick through the hole. This will be the candle's wick. Place a few candies in the bottom of the mold; pour a little wax in the mold. Keep adding candies and wax until the mold is full. Allow the wax to cool completely and invert the mold to release the candle. It can be placed in the freezer to harden more quickly; just tap the mold on a counter top, if needed, to help release the candle.

For a quick & easy gift, give an old-fashioned copper mold with the instructions for the Gelatin Mold Candle tucked inside.

Celebration Cake Carrier

Give a retro cake carrier a lively splash of color in minutes.

screwdriver
metal cake carrier
newspaper
spray primer
favorite color acrylic spray paint
acrylic enamel paints

paintbrushes
Optional: stencils
white paint marker
black permanent fine-line
   marker
matte acrylic sealer

Use a screwdriver to remove the knob from the cake carrier dome; set the cake carrier plate aside. In a well-ventilated area, cover a work surface with newspaper. Spray primer on the exterior of the dome; let dry. Coat dome with spray paint. When completely dry, top with a second coat and let dry again. Using enamel paints, freehand paint or use stencils to add fun designs. Triangles can easily become party hats, confetti squares are made with a small flat paintbrush or add dots by dipping a pencil eraser into paint. Use the white paint marker to write a cheery greeting. To make the lettering stand out, add black marker shadows around each letter. Let carrier dry completely, coat with matte sealer and then replace the knob. Be sure to hand wash only.

Celebrating a special anniversary, birthday or new addition to the family? Make this cake carrier a one-of-a-kind gift...it's sure to be a keepsake.

*☆ Use it up, wear it out,
make it do, or do without ☆*

Decoupage Step Stool

*Anything that holds special memories can be used
to create this one-of-a-kind keepsake.*

painted step stool
sandpaper
acrylic sealer
postcards, pressed flowers,
    photos or recipe cards

scissors
decoupage medium
foam brush
acrylic sealer

When using a flea market-find step stool, wash and dry it first to
remove any loose paint, sanding if necessary to get a smooth surface.
Coat with acrylic sealer to seal the surface. Make color copies of
postcards, pressed flowers, photos or recipe cards; cut out with
scissors and arrange, as desired, on step stool. Coat the back of each
with decoupage medium using a foam brush. Apply it to the seat of
the stool, smoothing with your fingers to remove any air bubbles.
Continue adding copies, but when overlapping images, let each dry
about 15 minutes before adding another layer. When all copies are
placed, top with three coats of acrylic sealer to protect them.

*Can't find a step stool?
No problem; use a
lampshade, bench,
cupboard or chair for
your decoupage project.*

Keepsake Frame

Pages from an old-fashioned children's cookbook make the sweetest photo mats to share with a friend.

picture frame
pencil
page from a vintage children's
 cookbook

utility knife or scissors
photo corners or a glue stick
photo to be framed

Remove the back from the picture frame; set aside. Use a pencil to lightly mark a square on the back of the book page where you'd like the photo to show through. Use a utility knife or scissors to carefully cut along the pencil line; discard the middle cut-out. Position the book page, right-side down, on the back of the glass. Smooth out any wrinkles. Use photo corners or a glue stick to secure the photo, face down, on the back of the book page. Turn frame over carefully to see lif the photo is showing through the cut-out as desired. Replace the frame back.

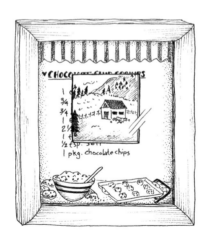

Try using color copies of favorite scrapbook pages for this Keepsake Frame...so sweet!

Colander Wind Chime

What a great way to recycle all that mismatched silverware!

5 pieces of silverware
mallet
c-clamp

power drill with 1/8-inch drill bit
fishing line
colander

Flatten each piece of silverware by placing them, one at a time, on a large flat, protected surface and pounding with the mallet. Next, secure each utensil to a table edge with a c-clamp. Using the 1/8-inch drill bit, drill through the center of each utensil handle. While drilling, be sure to press firmly so the drill doesn't move. Be careful as metal will be hot after drilling. Cut approximately a 10-inch length of fishing line for the center utensil or "clapper" of the chime. For the 4 other utensils, cut pieces of line approximately 8 inches long. Thread line through the drilled hole in each utensil, feed it through a pair of holes in the colander bottom and tie a knot at the ends. Add a length of fishing line through the the handles on each side of the colander to hang the finished wind chime.

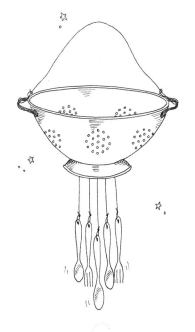

Almost anything can be used to make these wonderful wind chimes. Look for copper kettles, enamelware pans, silver sugar bowls or coffee urns...each one has its own appeal!

One-of-a-Kind Lampshade

With a little vintage fabric it's a snap to turn an ordinary lampshade into one that's extra special!

scissors
various fabric scraps
lampshade
foam brush

decoupage medium
Optional: ribbon, beaded trim, rick-rack, craft glue

Cut fabric into different shapes and place on lampshade until a desired pattern is achieved. Dip foam brush into decoupage medium, brush the backs of each piece of fabric and secure to lampshade; let dry. Once all fabric has been placed on the lampshade, brush decoupage medium over the entire surface of the lampshade and fabric pieces; let dry. If desired, finish the top and bottom edges of the lampshade with ribbon, beaded trim or rick-rack, secured in place with craft glue.

Giving this decoupaged lampshade an "antiqued" look is easy...just sponge on brown acrylic paint that's been thinned with water.

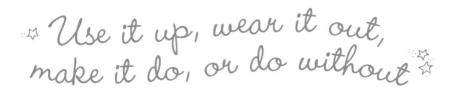
Ruffled Lap Blanket

Don't pass up those tag sale wool sweaters…they can easily be stitched into a one-of-a-kind blanket!

a selection of old wool sweaters
   in favorite colors
iron
ruler

cardboard
sewing machine
thread
scissors

Wash sweaters in hot water; tumble dry at the hottest setting and iron on a steam setting to remove any wrinkles. This process can always be repeated if the wool doesn't seem felted enough. Test wool by cutting a bit and pulling gently on the fibers to make sure it's not fraying easily…it shouldn't. Using ruler, create a 5-inch square from the cardboard. This will be the template for cutting the wool. Lay cardboard on wool and cut out 48 squares. Place 2 squares side-by-side, without overlapping them, and use the widest zig-zag stitch on a sewing machine to stitch down the center of the side-by-side edges. Continue adding squares until you have a row of 8 squares. Make 5 more rows of 8 squares, then stitch the rows together, one at a time, using the same zig-zag stitch on the sewing machine. When all rows are completely stitched together, finish the edges along the outside with a zig-zag stitch. Each square along with the outer edge, will pucker creating a pretty ruffle effect. Finished size will be 40"x30".

This lap blanket makes a great rainy day project with the kids. With just a few practice stitches, even a beginner can make one in no time.

Brown Sugar Scrub in a Jar

Small apothecary jars are everywhere at flea markets and come in lots of fun shapes and sizes. Filled with this scented sugar scrub, they'll make a really welcome gift!

wide-mouth glass jars and lids
1 c. brown sugar, packed
1/4 c. almond oil

1/2 t. vitamin E oil
6 to 8 drops scented essential oil

Thoroughly wash and dry jars; set aside to dry completely. In a large bowl, combine remaining ingredients until combined well. Pack into glass jars; secure lids. Makes approximately one cup.

Pint-size canning jars from the 1950's can also be filled with Brown Sugar Scrub. Their brightly colored lids add a fun splash of color!

Trinket Paperweight

The prettiest way to save some of those tiny collectibles you just can't part with.

shallow glass ashtray (without grooves)
decorative paper
lightweight cardboard
felt
craft glue
buttons, charms, tiny seashells, stamps or fabric snippets
pencil
scissors

Trace around the bottom of the ashtray on decorative paper; repeat with cardboard and felt. Glue felt to one side of the cardboard and the decorative paper to the other side; let dry. Add trinkets inside the ashtray and add a small amount of glue to the rim. Place the cardboard square, decorative-paper side down, on the rim; let dry. Allow to dry thoroughly before turning right-side up. When turned over, the objects inside will move about freely on top of the decorative-paper background.

Sometimes it's the larger souvenirs that really bring back special memories. Try placing a single seashell, starfish or postcard image inside a paperweight.

Charming Necklace

Buttons, charms and sewing box trims can become a beautiful necklace in almost no time at all.

18-inch length of ribbon
1 large charm or decorative
   button
needle

thread to match ribbon
an even number of smaller
   buttons or charms
jewelry closings

Lay ribbon flat and place large charm or button in the center. Use needle and thread to secure charm to ribbon. Stitch the remaining buttons or charms evenly around the remainder of the ribbon. Attach jewelry closings, available at craft stores, to the ribbon ends.

Thoughtful bridesmaids' gifts...use lengths of ribbon and vintage buttons to create charming bracelets.

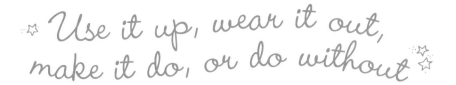
Bottle Cap Push Pins & Magnets

What a clever way to add personality to a bulletin board!

bottle caps
tacky craft glue

push pins
magnets

Turn bottle caps upside down and add a dollop of tacky craft glue. Immediately press a push pin head or magnet into the glue and hold until secure. Continue with remaining caps.

Fabric Yo-Yo Push Pins & Magnets

Because it's exceptionally strong, button thread is a must.

fabric scrap
3-inch diameter drinking glass
pencil
scissors
needle

button thread
tacky craft glue
flat-top tacks
magnets

Place fabric, right-side down, on a flat surface. Set the drinking glass on top and trace around it with a pencil. Repeat as many times as desired. Cut out circles; set aside. Thread needle and turn under raw edge of circle 1/8 inch, taking small running stitches. Pull thread to gather yo-yo into a tight circle with the right side of the fabric facing out. Secure end of thread to hold gathers in place. Place a dab of tacky craft glue on the flat side of the fabric and quickly secure to the tack head or magnet; let dry. One, 3-inch fabric circle will equal one, 1-1/2 inch diameter yo-yo.

Framed Note Board

*Old-fashioned picture and window frames are everywhere
at flea markets...create something new with them!*

large picture frame or window
    frame
tape measure
scissors
fabric

thin corkboard
utility knife
spray adhesive
tacks or small nails
hammer

Carefully clean frame to remove any dust or dirt. Place frame,
right-side down, on a flat, protected surface and measure opening. Add
1/4-inch edge to allow for overlap. Cut fabric to measurements; repeat
with corkboard using utility knife. Coat corkboard with spray adhesive
and quickly lay fabric on top, smoothing edges to remove wrinkles.
Center corkboard, fabric-side down, on the back of the frame. Use
tacks or hammer small nails around the edges to secure
the corkboard to the frame.

*Try securing a dry erase board to the back of a
divided window frame for a new spin with
a vintage look!*

Heart Make-Do

Years ago women made pincushions, called make-do's then, using oil lamps and candlesticks. Try this clever idea for creating your own unique pincushion!

2 8-inch squares of wool felt, quilt top or cotton calico fabric
6-inch heart-shaped cookie cutter or template
pencil
sewing machine
scissors

polyester fiberfill
quilting thread
needle
craft glue
candlestick
Optional: old buttons, charms or beads

Place right-sides of fabric together, and trace heart onto the fabric with a pencil. Sew directly on the pencil line leaving bottom of heart open and wide enough to insert the candlestick. Trim seam 1/4 inch and clip curves before turning the heart right-side out. Stuff heart firmly with polyester fiberfill. While stuffing heart, flatten with your hand. Thread needle with quilting thread. Turn under the raw edge, at the bottom of heart, 1/4 inch and use a small running stitch around the base. Leave thread tail, do not knot yet. Put glue around the top of the candlestick and insert candlestick into the base of the heart; pull heart over the top of the candlestick and pull thread to tighten. Knot thread. Let dry for several hours before embellishing your heart with old buttons, charms or beads.

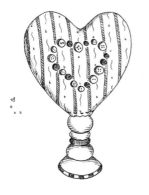

Have a ball making pincushions in any shape...stars, flowers, moons and pumpkins are just a few ideas!

Relaxing Lavender Pillow

Filled with the clean scent of lavender, a freshly starched flea-market find pillowcase is so nice at bedtime.

scissors
millet or buckwheat hull pillow
funnel
2 c. dried lavender buds

needle
thread
vintage pillowcase

Using scissors, carefully undo about a one-inch length of the seam from one corner of the millet or buckwheat hull pillow. Use the funnel to pour lavender buds into pillow. Stitch seam closed; gently shake from side to side to combine. Slip pillow into pillowcase; stitch pillowcase closed, if desired.

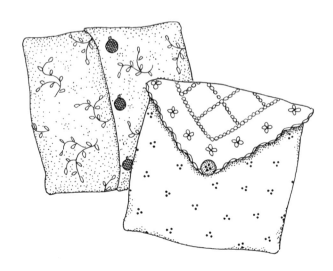

Easily found at decorating stores, buckwheat or millet hull pillows provide great neck support while sleeping. Add any favorite dried flower or herb to the pillow...try using rose petals, scented geranium or mint leaves.

Index

Index

Index

old-fashioned goodness ... for today!

delicious dinners • just like Mom's • (only easier) • piping hot • come & get it! • make it easy • carefree cooking • it's a snap • old-fashioned goodness ... for today!

U.S. to Metric Recipe Equivalents

Volume Measurements

1/4 teaspoon	1 mL
1/2 teaspoon	2 mL
1 teaspoon	5 mL
1 tablespoon = 3 teaspoons	15 mL
2 tablespoons = 1 fluid ounce	30 mL
1/4 cup	60 mL
1/3 cup	75 mL
1/2 cup = 4 fluid ounces	125 mL
1 cup = 8 fluid ounces	250 mL
2 cups = 1 pint =16 fluid ounces	500 mL
4 cups = 1 quart	1 L

Weights

1 ounce	30 g
4 ounces	120 g
8 ounces	225 g
16 ounces = 1 pound	450 g

Oven Temperatures

300° F	150° C
325° F	160° C
350° F	180° C
375° F	190° C
400° F	200° C
450° F	230° C

Baking Pan Sizes

Square	
8x8x2 inches	2 L = 20x20x5 cm
9x9x2 inches	2.5 L = 23x23x5 cm
Rectangular	
13x9x2 inches	3.5 L = 33x23x5 cm

Loaf	
9x5x3 inches	2 L = 23x13x7 cm
Round	
8x1-1/2 inches	1.2 L = 20x4 cm
9x1-1/2 inches	1.5 L = 23x4 cm

Find Gooseberry Patch
wherever you are!

www.gooseberrypatch.com

Call us toll-free at 1·800·854·6673